CW01024086

ART NOUVEAU FASHION

Junior 889

ART NOUVEAU FASHION

CLARE ROSE

V&A Publishing

First published by V&A Publishing, 2014

V&A Publishing
Victoria and Albert Museum
South Kensington
London SW7 2RL
www.vandapublishing.com

Distributed in North America by Abrams, an imprint of ABRAMS

© Victoria and Albert Museum, London
The moral right of the author has been asserted.

ISBN 978 1 85177 802 7
Library of Congress Catalog Control Number 2014932322

10 9 8 7 6 5 4 3 2
2018 2017 2016 2015

A catalogue record for this book is available from the British Library.
All rights reserved. No part of this publication may be reproduced, stored in a retrieval system, or transmitted
in any form or by any means electronic, mechanical, photocopying, recording or otherwise, without the written
permission of the publishers.

Every effort has been made to seek permission to reproduce those images whose copyright does not reside
with the V&A, and we are grateful to the individuals and institutions who have assisted in this task. Any
omissions are entirely unintentional, and the details should be addressed to V&A Publishing.

Designed by Schober Design
Copy-edited by Rachel Malig
Index by Hilary Bird
New V&A photography by Paul Robins, V&A Photographic Studio
Printed in China

Front jacket/cover illustration: see pl.22 (detail)
Back jacket/cover illustration: see pl.95
Frontispiece: see pl.16

V&A Publishing
Supporting the world's leading
museum of art and design,
the Victoria and Albert
Museum, London

CONTENTS

INTRODUCTION
ART NOUVEAU

—

Art Nouveau was a style in decorative art and architecture prevalent between 1890 and 1914, with manifestations in North America and throughout Europe, including Russia. This broad geographical and chronological spread led to a striking diversity in style, but it was characterized by flowing lines, natural forms, the use of symbolism, exotic influences and innovative approaches to materials. Such were the varied influences – and even internal contradictions – that one designer commented in 1904:

> Traces of decadence, primitive motives, attenuated Pre-Raphaelitism, Japanese influence – all are summarized. One sees even the electric wire and insulator motive as decorative units ... l'Art Nouveau is replete with beauty of line, grace of form, and freedom. It is a sympathetic style and in its vast rendering is full of repose and quiet unobtrusive beauty. It is Art pure and simple, untrammeled by convention and therefore, in a sense, original.[1]

As it was a style rather than a formal movement, there is also some disagreement about the relationship between Art Nouveau and groups of artists such as the Fauves, the Viennese Secession or the Glasgow School of Art. These groups, though they presented work in differing styles, shared some characteristics that were fundamental to Art Nouveau, notably the use of esoteric symbolism linked to modern products and commercial practices. There have been many discussions about the demarcation lines between Art Nouveau and the styles that preceded and followed it, in particular Arts and Crafts, Modernism and Art Deco. In fact, Art Nouveau combined features of all three: the exquisite hand workmanship and use of natural forms of Arts and Crafts; the querying of conventional materials, forms and practices associated with Modernism; and the surface patterning of Art Deco. However, Art Nouveau had a very different attitude to the other movements, which insisted on truth to materials and aimed to provide good design for all. Instead, Art Nouveau was, even in its most public manifestations such as advertising posters, wilfully elitist, with the products on offer obscured by writhing tendrils or represented only symbolically. It was also infused with decadent sexuality, with femmes fatales a leitmotif in literature, music, art and decoration.

Women were of central importance in Art Nouveau, as subjects of art and commerce: 'whether for a railway, absinthe, corsets, coffee, electric lighting, a chemical lab, exhibition of art or even Russian shoe oil, the artists exploited the image of the sensuous, beautiful young woman in fashionable dress and with

1
Alphonse Mucha, 'Job Cigarette Papers'
Colour lithograph poster,

51.5 x 39 cm
Paris, 1898
V&A: E.260-1921

exotic hairstyle'.[2] These images were often sexually provocative, both in their subjects and depictions, as with Alphonse Mucha's poster showing a scantily clad young woman enjoying smoking, a pastime seen as a masculine privilege (pl.1). Other poster images highlighted the rise of independent working women, who were beginning to challenge the male stranglehold on white-collar jobs and professions (pl.2).

Women's role in creating art, however, was restricted by both the regulations and the attitudes of the artistic establishment. As the reviewer of an 1892 exhibition of 'Les Arts de la femme' stated, 'What a woman suggests is worth more than what she conceives . . . [she is] an inexhaustible orchestrator of worldly elegance.'[3] Chief among the forms of 'worldly elegance' was fashionable dress, which differed from other forms of decorative art in being visible to all, not just visitors to the owner's home. It also needed to be regularly renewed, allowing consumers to demonstrate their taste – and that they had the means to gratify it – on a seasonal or monthly basis.

2
Lucien Faure, 'The Empire Typewriter'
Colour lithograph poster,
150 x 96.5 cm
London, 1897
V&A: Circ.586–1962

DRESS AS AN ART FORM

One of the distinctive aspects of Art Nouveau was its integration of fashionable clothing into the decorative arts. This was recognized at the time: 'We live in one of the rare periods in history when all of the arts, aiming at the same goal of renewal, work together to produce pieces that make up a harmonious ensemble.'[4] From the 1870s, the Arts and Crafts and Aesthetic movements had advocated 'artistic' dress, which aspired to the status of art by being timeless, and by prioritizing the aesthetic choices of the wearer over social convention. Artistic dress was linked to the movement for dress reform and was usually designed to be worn without conventional corsets, limiting its adoption to a small coterie. The construction and decoration of artistic garments was taught in art colleges, notably Glasgow and Vienna, where it reached a wider public through exhibitions and publications (see Chapter 6).[5]

What was new in Art Nouveau was the discussion of garments and accessories by commercial firms as works of art. Some of these firms had an ambiguous relationship to conventional fashion, such as the house of Paul Poiret, which produced garments that embodied many of the aims of dress reformers while claiming the status of haute couture. It was Poiret who was cited as the epitome of the 'art of the dress', hailed by the art critic Paul Cornu in 1911:

3
Siegfried Bing, The Art Nouveau Bing Pavilion, Exposition Universelle 1900, Paris
From *Deutsche Kunst und Dekoration*, 1901
V&A: NAL

for it is an art, do not doubt it, not only because it calls on the support of other arts ... but because it emphasizes human forms, which are such a fruitful source of inspiration for designers, and because, like all decorative arts, it considers beauty in relationship to its setting.[6]

The designs of couturiers were also discussed both as art and as part of an industry that was economically important, particularly in France. At the Exposition Universelle 1900 in Paris, generally credited with popularizing Art Nouveau for a global audience, the main entrance was crowned by a statue representing the fashion trade – La Parisienne – in robes designed by the leading couturier, Madame Paquin. The catalogue of the display organized by the association of French couturiers for this exhibition argued that, in directing not only the consumption but also the production of textiles and trimmings, French fashion should be counted as an industry of global importance.[7] The lavish decoration and exquisite trimmings illustrated in this book support the claim for these garments to be seen as works of decorative art.

The Art Nouveau aesthetic was one that aimed at a '*gesamtkunstwerk*' or complete work of art, in which works in different media or scales formed part of a harmonious whole rather than competing for attention. This attitude was fostered by leaders of taste such as Siegfried Bing, whose pavilion at the Exposition Universelle 1900 showed entire rooms fitted out with the latest wall-coverings, furniture, carpets and *objets d'art*. In some cases the

4
Eugène Gaillard, 'Chambre à Coucher', The Art Nouveau Bing Pavilion, Exposition Universelle 1900, Paris
From *The Art Journal*, London, 1901
V&A: NAL

furnishings and room décor were so closely related that it would be unthinkable to install one without the other, as in the bedroom by Eugène Gaillard exhibited by Bing (pl.4). One might expect the patrons who commissioned designs such as these to be equally discerning in their choice of clothing; Bing suggested as much in the façade of his pavilion, which was decorated with frescoes of elegant women whose fashionable clothing was stylized so that it resembled the architecture that framed it (pl.3). Indeed some Art Nouveau architectural projects contained elements so extravagantly decorative that their swirls and curlicues might have been taken from the embroidery of a dress, or the feathers in a hat, as with the lobby of the Castel Béranger (1894–8), designed by Hector Guimard (pl.5).

Contemporary critics saw the correspondence between modern styles in architecture and dress; the architect Hermann Muthesius wrote of Charles Rennie Mackintosh's clean white interiors, 'an ordinary person . . . would look out of place wearing simple working clothes in this fairy tale world'.[8] An article that reviewed Glasgow projects by Mackintosh and others probably referred to him when it wrote:

Even feminine attire has not escaped the attention of the modern artist; with some recent schemes of decoration he has indicated the design and colour of the gowns to be worn, so that no disturbing element might mar the unity of the conception.[9]

5
Hector Guimard,
'Entrance Hall'
From *Le Castel Béranger:*
œuvre de Hector Guimard,
architecte, professeur à
l'Ecole nationale des arts
décoratifs
Paris, 1898
V&A: NAL

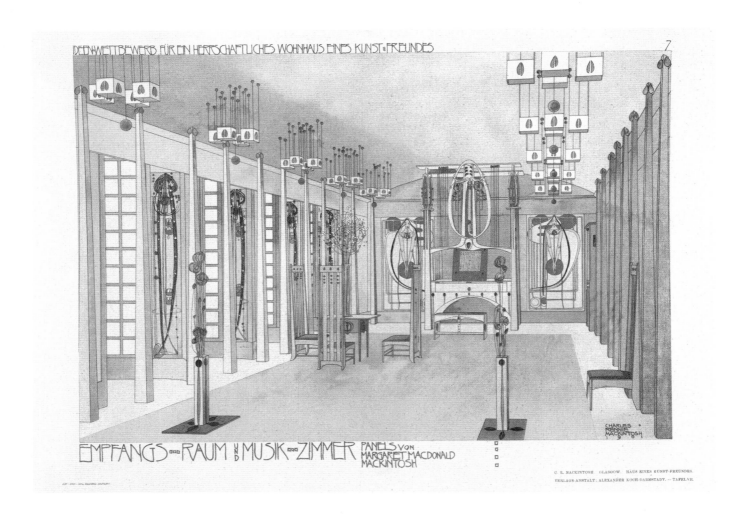

This uncompromising vision may be one of the reasons why some of Mackintosh's projects for private clients remained unbuilt, as with his 'House for An Art Lover' (pl.6).

ART NOUVEAU FASHION

The dress historian Lou Taylor, commenting on the V&A exhibition 'International Art Nouveau 1890–1914', pointed out the danger of judging *fin-de-siècle* objects by our own standards. Isolating single pieces in museum vitrines can be misleading, as they were designed to be seen in ensembles where dress, jewels, hair and body all responded to each other.[10] There is also a danger of discussing individual fashion designers in isolation from their artistic and cultural context, and from the structure of their businesses. It is salutary to leaf through exhibition catalogues and magazines from 1890 to 1914 and see how much space is given to couture houses that have since faded into obscurity: Aine-Montaillé, Beer, Barroin, Bonnaire, Drécoll,

6
Charles Rennie Mackintosh and Margaret Macdonald Mackintosh, 'Reception and Music Room'
From Hermann Muthesius, *Haus eines Kunstfreundes* Darmstadt, 1902
V&A: NAL

Doeuillet, Ernst Raudnitz, Blanche Lebouvier, Ney Soeurs and Vaganey were all respected couturiers in 1900, but are little-known now.[11] However, it is clear from the wealth of illustrated magazines dedicated to fashion, and from the fashion columns in every newspaper, that there was a highly effective network for disseminating fashion information both within the trade and to consumers.

At international exhibitions, from Chicago in 1893 to Turin in 1911, fashion was increasingly part of the attraction. In addition to the cases of mass-produced boots and corsets in the industrial sections, there were special installations that presented the fashions of the moment – or of the past – on lifelike wax figures in lavish room settings. These provided inspiration for both retailers and consumers, and helped to promote the international trade in fashion. Thus fashion innovations originated by an individual designer would be speedily evaluated by competitors and either adapted or rejected. Moreover, the reach of fashion was wider than ever, as ready-to-wear clothing, previously derided as one-size-fits-all 'slops', and made-to-measure haute couture were seen as belonging to the same fashion system. Designs by couture houses such as Lucile were worn onstage or in movies and illustrated in mass-circulation newspapers, while ready-to-wear manufacturers offered garments with so many variations in fabric and trimming that they became a form of 'wholesale bespoke'.[12]

The boundaries between masculine and feminine clothing were also being eroded during this period, as women adopted a range of tailored garments: first practical overcoats and waterproofs, then skirt suits worn with a stiffly starched collar and tie, and even, for some sports, knee breeches. Male dandies were also seeking to extend the range of colours and styles permissible in fashionable clothing, giving rise to accusations of effeminacy.[13] At the same time, military and court uniforms provided officially sanctioned opportunities for the wearing of bright colours and lavish embroidery. These uniforms later became a key component of the re-evaluation of *fin-de-siècle* style by the 1960s counter-culture. The transition from the hard-edged modernism of the early 1960s to the more relaxed and poetic styles of the 1970s was driven by small boutiques in London and California specializing in original and reproduction Art Nouveau artefacts.

The Art Nouveau revival of the 1960s was not purely a reaction to the prevailing space-age aesthetic. It also recognized in Art Nouveau an alternative approach to modernity. In 1900 fashion design embraced the new technologies of its time; the exaggerated curves of corsets and the ever-higher heels of fashionable boots would not have been possible without processes such as machine-sewing and steam moulding. Electric lighting was used to illuminate fashion boutiques, and to facilitate staged spectacles that put the female body on show, from Loïe Fuller's veiled dances to the first fashion films, such as *Kinemacolor Fashion Gazette* (1913). This blending of technological innovation and sensuous pleasure helps to explain why Art Nouveau fashion still has the capacity to surprise and inspire.

CHAPTER I
DESIGNING FASHION

—

The period from 1890 to 1914 was the apogee of the Paris couture house, a relatively recent development. There had been a few high-profile fashion designers before 1850, such as Rose Bertin, 'Minister of Fashion' to Queen Marie Antoinette from 1774 to 1792, and Hippolyte Leroy, who supplied gowns to Danish royalty in the 1840s.[1] However, dressmakers, milliners and tailors were largely anonymous, making up garments following the suggestions, and the fabric choices, of their clients.

From 1870, a new generation of designers emerged, who sourced exclusive fabrics, designed styles to show them off, and provided accessories to match.

7 opposite
Paquin, design for evening dress with exotic embroidery
From album for Winter 1911
Pen and gouache
Paris, 1911
V&A: E.2051-1957

8 right
Worth, tailored wool costume
Paris, c.1910
V&A: AAD/4/26/1990

By 1900 individual designers were credited as the originators of a range of seasonal designs that were publicized in the press and shown on house models before they were made up for clients. They acted as figureheads for couture houses, large commercial organizations with multiple branches and hundreds of employees. In 1900 the House of Worth had six branches, each employing over 400 people.[2] In these large-scale operations the special expertise of the founding designers – lingerie and lace (Callot sisters), tailoring and sportswear (Redfern) or rich fabrics (Worth) – was subsumed by the need to offer a full range of services to clients (pl.8).

A 1910 volume, *Les Créateurs de la mode*, included photographs showing a broad similarity between the leading Paris designers in terms of the types of garments on offer – tailored 'costumes' and sportswear, fitted day dresses, formal evening gowns and wraps, informal tea gowns and lingerie, millinery and accessories – and in the luxury and refinement of their showrooms.[3] Design innovations – in cut, fabric or trim – were swiftly adopted by competitors and by smaller firms such as Madame Handley Seymour of London, who copied Paris 'models' for clients (pls 10 and 11).

Copies of the latest Paris styles were also available from large department stores, based on model garments or on sketches purchased from Paris.[4] Department stores developed in the 1850s in Paris and London when retailers of fabric or of specialist articles such as baby clothes added counters selling garments and novelties.[5] Jay's of London, which had started in 1841 as a

9
**Jays of London,
evening dress**
Satin, with metallic
embroidery (Turkish)
on silk
London, c.1908
V&A: T.193–1970

10 *above*
Poiret, 'Sorbet' evening ensemble, worn by Denise Poiret
Satin, bead-embroidered, fur trim
Paris, 1913
V&A: T.385–1976

11 *right*
Madame Handley Seymour after Poiret, fashion design, 'Sorbet'
Watercolour, 34 x 25 cm
London, 1913
V&A: E.916–1958

'mourning warehouse' providing garments for the recently bereaved, was by 1900 offering all types of clothing, including evening gowns incorporating gold embroidery from Turkey (pl.9).[6] By 1900, stores such as Lord and Taylor of New York, Marshall Fields of Chicago, the Printemps of Paris and Marshall and Snelgrove of London were offering a full range of services, from off-the-peg garments, to special made-to-measure commissions, to services such as dry cleaning (pl.22). In addition, there were many chains of stores and mail-order retailers offering stylish ready-to-wear clothing that adapted distinctive features of the new season's lines – the balloon sleeve of 1895, the narrow skirt of 1908 – to the demands of mass-production.[7]

Clothing was traded internationally on a large scale: in 1914 the French textile and clothing industries generated over 33 per cent of all export revenue and employed a third of the French labour force.[8] There was also an international trade in images and instructions for making up fashionable garments, presented in books and periodicals addressed to tailoring and dressmaking professionals, as well as to clients.

The intense competition within and between different branches of the fashion industry created a tension for couturiers between creating distinctive work that maintained their reputation as fashion leaders, and providing clothes suited to the needs of their clients. Some of their publicity and reputation management strategies are discussed in Chapter 3, and relationships between designers and clients in Chapter 4; this chapter will focus on the design and production of garments, starting with an overview of some of the key couture houses of this period.

HOUSE OF WORTH

Charles Frederick Worth (1825–95), often described as the 'father of haute couture', was responsible for two innovations whose effects far outlasted even his most striking designs.[9] The first was his assertion of the primacy of his own creative vision over the preferences of all but his most exalted clients: 'The women who come to me want to ask for my ideas, not to follow their own . . . If I tell them they are suited, they need no further evidence. My signature to their gown suffices!'[10] His role as 'dictator of fashion' ensured that his garments were associated with his name rather than that of his clients – from the late 1880s, they were even 'signed' with a facsimile of his signature on the waistband.[11] His second innovation was to license copies of his designs by selected retailers, such as Lord and Taylor of New York, with sets of the appropriate fabrics and trimmings.[12] Together, these practices commoditized fashion designs as items with a value separate from the garments they inspired.

The House of Worth was founded in 1857 in Paris, and soon gained the Empress Eugénie and leading members of her court as clients. Worth's training in a drapery business was evident in his provision of rich fabrics, some woven exclusively for him (pl.12). Different types of clothes were displayed in rooms

12
Worth, evening dress
Silk velvet on satin ground, woven 'à disposition'
Paris, 1898–1900
Metropolitan Museum of Art, New York

13
**Enrico Sacchetti, fashion
plate for Worth**
Gouache on paper
Paris, 1913
V&A: E.22191-1957

14
Worth, evening wrap
Embroidered silk,
velvet, tassels
Paris, c.1909
V&A: T.207–1970

with appropriate lighting: daylight for outdoor clothes, gaslight for evening gowns.[13] This luxury was not cheap, with dresses costing upwards of 1,600 FF in 1868 (the Louvre's budget for acquiring new works that year was 7,000 FF).[14] In the 1870s, C.F. Worth was joined in the business by his sons Jean-Philippe (1856–1926) as lead designer, and Gaston (1853–1924) as business manager; these two ensured the continuity of the house after the founder's death in 1895, supported from 1910 by Gaston's son Jean-Charles. There was a period of expansion, with branches set up in the seaside resorts of Dinard and Biarritz, and in London (1902). In the Exposition Universelle 1900, Gaston Worth was Président de classe for the clothing category of exhibits, and was awarded the Légion d'honneur for his efforts.

After 1900 the firm engaged new designers – including Paul Poiret, who was with Worth from 1901 to 1903 – but these were not accepted by their more conservative customers and by 1904 the firm was downsizing its premises.[15] Nevertheless, its established tradition and its ability to follow, if not to lead, changing trends, enabled the House of Worth to continue in business until 1954, when it merged with Paquin (pls 13 and 14).

Maison Paquin

The Exposition Universelle 1900 marked a turning point in the reputations of the Paris couture houses: while Gaston Worth was in charge of clothing as a whole, the selection of couture garments was entrusted to his rival Jeanne

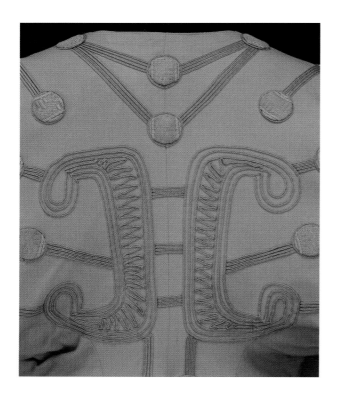

15
Paquin, day ensemble, 'Sybille' (detail)
Wool with silk braiding
Paris, 1906
V&A: T.73–1967

Paquin (1869–1936). From humble origins, she had trained as a dressmaker and established her own house in 1891, funded by her new husband, the banker Isidore Paquin. This was so successful that by 1896 they were able to set up a London office, followed by establishments in New York (1912), Madrid (1914) and Buenos Aires (1915).[16] Paquin's establishment was such a renowned Parisian sight that it was represented in paintings showing both fashionable clients crowding the salon and smartly dressed staff leaving at the end of the day.[17]

Like Worth, Paquin often referenced historic dress through details carefully selected to fit with current trends. Around 1900 she re-examined the styles of a century earlier, adopting first the masculine lapels and waistcoats of 1790, then

16
Paquin, design for evening dress with exotic accessories
From album for Winter 1911
Pen and gouache
Paris, 1911
V&A: E.2060–1957

the raised waistlines of 1800.[18] However, these references were incorporated into a contemporary silhouette, and were refreshed by the use of contemporary fabrics and trimmings. Unexpected combinations of fabrics, such as fur trim on evening gowns, were a hallmark of the house (pls 7 and 15).

Paquin's designs also showed bold use of colour and contrasts: a surviving 1898 ensemble in black silk is trimmed with scrolls of magenta silk appliqué,[19] while a day dress from 1905 in cherry red wool with bold embroidery may represent the shade later known as 'Paquin Red'.[20] From 1908, Paquin presented garments in the latest 'fauve' colours and 'directoire' cut, modified for ease of wearing with side slits or draped panels in narrow skirts, and white collars and cuffs to relieve intense colours (pl.16).[21] She anticipated the modernist simplification of dress codes by producing day-to-evening ensembles as early as 1913.[22] Paquin's understanding of how much novelty her clientele would accept was one of her greatest assets; as the *New York Times* wrote of her in 1911, 'She has introduced more lasting fashions than probably any other woman in Paris, for she has had the good sense never to be extreme.'[23]

Lucile Ltd
—

One of Paquin's greatest rivals was Lucy Wallace, later Lady Duff-Gordon (1863–1935), who opened in business as 'Lucile' in London in 1893.[24] With no formal training or experience, her chief asset was her circle of wealthy and artistic friends, including her sister, the scandalous novelist Elinor Glyn. However, she soon demonstrated an ability to layer delicate fabrics and trimmings to produce effects that were refined rather than overwhelming. This can be seen in her surviving sample book for the 1905 summer season, containing coloured sketches surrounded by swatches of the fabrics and trimmings proposed.[25] This enabled clients to envisage the effect of the finished garment, and to request any changes they required – and also aided stock control in the workrooms. By 1911 the business had expanded to New York and Paris, with a Chicago branch added in 1915. Her 'gowns of emotion' were rich in sensual and romantic references, heightened by titles such as 'The tender grace of a day that is dead' (pl.17).[26]

Others made reference to exotic dress, with sari-like drapes and Egyptian-style beading (pl.18). Lucile was also known for her luxurious lingerie and informal garments, shown to clients in the boudoir-like 'Rose Room'.[27] However, she produced a full range of garments, including tailored suits in wool tweed or serge, as well as designing for movies such as *The Perils of Pauline* (1914).[28]

17 *above*
**Lucile, 'The tender grace
of a day that is dead'**
From album for Lucile Ltd,
Autumn 1905
Drawing with watercolour
and fabric swatches,
30.5 x 24.5 cm
London, 1905
V&A: T.89A-1986

18 *right*
**Henri Manuel for Lucile,
negligee ensemble posed
in garden**
Paris, *c.*1910
V&A: AAD/2008/6/28

Maison Poiret

—

The career of Paul Poiret (1879–1944) illustrates some of the contradictions inherent in the couture system before 1914. The son of a textile merchant, he worked for the couture houses of Raudnitz (1896–8), Doucet (1898–1900) and Worth (1901–3), before setting up under his own name. His conventional training, and his experience of working with clients including the actresses Réjane and Sarah Bernhardt, were belied by the unconventionality of his designs. While at Worth he created wraps based on Japanese kimonos, and his own designs were notable for their use of large draped panels rather than intricately cut and seamed segments (see pl.69).[29] The rejection of the structures and boned stiffening used in contemporary fashion highlighted the beauty of the surface fabric, which moved fluidly over the body of the wearer (pl.19). Many of Poiret's most advanced designs were conceived for his wife Denise, whose boyishly slim figure did not need the support garments worn by more conventional beauties; even so, their lightweight construction was considered scandalously revealing.

Equally shocking was Poiret's promotion of Middle-Eastern ensembles with long tunics over full divided skirts or 'harem pants'. Poiret was not alone in this; Callot Soeurs (founded 1895) had produced lounging pyjamas from as early as 1909 (see pl.70). In February 1911 '*jupes culottes*' were adopted as outdoor garb by a number of other Paris and London design houses, and caused a commotion when worn at public events such as the races. The fashion, and the sensationalism with which it was treated, were mocked by a cartoon in the English magazine *Punch*: 'She dressed herself in the latest mode/And left her house in the Brompton Road/To popularise the harem kit/But she found that nobody noticed it/And the ribald laughter she hoped to hear/Never assailed her wakeful ear.'[30] The controversy was inflamed by Poiret's suggestion in an interview that the garment's reference to the harem should be emphasized by 'ankle-bandages incrusted with precious stones'.[31]

Poiret was deeply influenced by the arrival in Paris of Serge Diaghilev's Ballets Russes in 1909, with scenarios recreating exotic cultures from Central Asia (*Prince Igor, Firebird*) and the Near East (*Cleopatra, Schéhérazade*). As important for him was their promotion of consistency in design, with music, choreography, costumes and sets carefully considered in terms of the total effect.[32] The pursuit of a total design scheme was evident in Poiret's work from early on, and he kept close control on publicity, collaborating with graphic artists to produce *Les Robes de Paul Poiret racontées par Paul Iribe* (Paris, 1908) and *Les Choses de Paul Poiret vues par Georges Lepape* (Paris, 1911) (see pl.114). The 1908 volume was sent unsolicited to Queen Mary of England as a leader of fashionable society; its scantily draped figures were seen as indecent and the designer was firmly instructed to send no more communications.[33] The following year, Poiret was again at the centre of a scandal when Margot Asquith, the wife of the British Prime Minister, invited him to show his fashions at the official residence, 10 Downing Street. British clothing manufacturers were

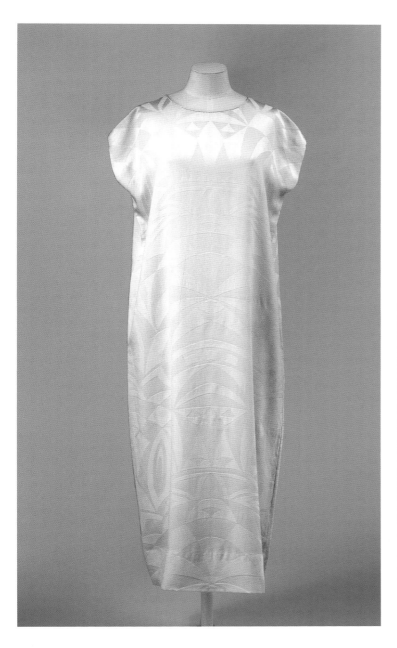

19 *above*
Poiret, 'Robe de minute' dress, worn by Denise Poiret
Figured silk satin, chiffon lining
Paris, 1911
V&A: T.118–1975

20 *right*
Poiret, 'La Perse' coat, worn by Denise Poiret, textile by Raoul Dufy
Block-printed cotton velvet, fur trim
Paris, 1911
Metropolitan Museum of Art, New York

incensed at the preference shown to a foreigner – the more so given the avant-garde nature of his designs.[34]

In 1913, Poiret produced an ensemble called 'Sorbet', which referenced a variety of orientalist sources, with a kimono-sleeved bodice flowing into a wired tunic based on Persian miniatures, worn over a draped skirt referencing Turkish trousers. This design was surprisingly successful, as evidenced by the survival of several variants by Poiret himself, and its inclusion in an album from a London house specializing in couture copies (pls 10 and 11).[35] Poiret's worldwide reputation reached its zenith in 1913, when a tour of the United States drew audiences of up to 60,000 per week, and both the designer and his wife were profiled at length in *Vogue*. However, this tour also revealed major problems with piracy, as Poiret's simple shift dresses were copied without acknowledgement by major retailers, and even his distinctive orientalist costumes were attributed to Leon Bakst (1866–1924), designer for the Ballets Russes.[36]

STRUCTURES AND SURFACES

With the increasing promotion of fashionable trends in news media, and increasing competition from the ready-to-wear trade, couturiers struggled to maintain an aura of exclusivity and prestige. One of their main selling points was their personalized service, offering garments conceived and fitted for a specific client. However, the internationalization of fashion, and the pressure to create new ensembles at short notice, meant that corners were cut – designs were duplicated, and garments hastily assembled. This was especially the case with ball gowns made for a single use; tailored coats and skirts, intended to last a season, would be more strongly constructed. The bodice of the Lucile gown 'Carresaute' is made from delicate layers of chiffon, lace and embroidery; an interior view shows that some of the trimmings are only tacked on, and the construction seams have been hastily altered (pl.21).[37] As there would have been several layers of washable underwear and a corset between the wearer and the dress lining, the quality of the interior finish would not have been so important.

One method of assuring exclusivity was to work with specially selected textiles; the figured velvets and brocades used by the House of Worth can identify their garments even when a label is lacking (pl.12). With a very different aesthetic but a similar rationale, Paul Poiret set up the 'Atelier Martine' in 1911 to produce bright, peasant-styled textile designs for him alone (see pl.110).[38] He also collaborated with fine artists such as Raoul Dufy to create large-scale block-printed textiles that offset the increasing simplicity of his garments (pl.20).[39] However, the economics of commissioning yardage meant that it was usually produced in quantities that would make several garments, perhaps in different colours, undermining the exclusivity of each example.[40] Thus, some clients insisted on using their own fabrics for special occasions, like Queen Alexandra at her 1902 coronation (see Chapter 4).

Alternatively, combining materials and trimmings allowed for variation between garments, as seen in an opera cloak by Worth of silk damask, trimmed with toning silk chiffon and contrasting lace to create luxurious textures (pl.24). Judiciously applied embroidery could also create the impression of a specially woven textile, allowing middle-market retailers to follow couture trends. An opera cloak from the London department store Marshall and Snelgrove used felt appliqué and silk embroidery to place the cow parsley plants popular for avant-garde jewellery in a sweeping arrangement from hem to neck (pl.22). The most luxurious garments had surfaces completely encrusted with carefully executed handwork: artificial flowers, fabric appliqué, beads, sequins and embroideries (pl.23). A 1910 evening gown by Callot Soeurs has a net tunic with scrolls of sequinned foliage carefully placed to lead the viewer's eye around the figure of the wearer; the delicacy of the fabric, and the limited use of the finished gown, add to the extravagance of the whole (pl.25). Equally lavish decoration was incorporated into theoretically washable 'lingerie' gowns, whose delicate openwork made them exceptionally fragile. An example from 1904–8 is hand-stitched from countless strips of machine- and hand-made lace, some of them specially worked to form the curves of the garment pieces (pl.26).

21
Lucile, 'Carresaute' evening dress (bodice detail)
Silk chiffon, taffeta, embroidered net, and metallic embroidery
London, 1905
V&A: T.42-2007

Robe Empire peau de Cygne
Modèle de Boué Sœurs

22 opposite
**Marshall and Snelgrove,
opera coat**
Velvet, silk embroidery,
felt appliqué
London, 1895–1900
V&A: T.49–1962

23 right
**Boué Soeurs, evening
dress**
Plate from *Les Toilettes de
la collectivité de la Couture,
Exposition universelle
internationale de 1900*
Paris, 1900
V&A: NAL

Prior to 1914, international couture firms were in competition with each other and with high-end suppliers of ready-to-wear such as department stores. They strove to maintain their reputation for innovation without being so extreme as to alienate their key clients. They aimed to provide a personalized service, while the pressure of executing orders in time for key social events, and of supplying clients at a distance, led to a degree of standardization. When examined closely, the histories of major firms show similarities that belie rival houses' claims to uniqueness.

24
Worth, opera cloak (detail)
Silk damask, silk chiffon, machine lace
Paris, 1895–1900
V&A: T.86–1991

25 *above*
Callot Soeurs, evening dress (detail)
Silk, machine lace, sequinned net
Paris, 1910–14
Metropolitan Museum of Art, New York

26 *right*
Day dress (detail)
Cotton lawn, crochet and machine lace
France (possibly), 1904–08
V&A: T.107–1939

CHAPTER 2

JEWELLERY & ACCESSORIES

—

As the prevailing ethos of Art Nouveau fashion was that the whole ensemble was a complete work of art, it followed that accessories assumed a hitherto unprecedented importance. Art Nouveau jewellery was often figurative rather than abstract, representing both conventionally beautiful (peacocks and flowers) and more challenging items (insects and demons) in a wide range of precious and semi-precious materials (pl.27). The theorist Paul Escritt noted, 'Given that the traditional role of jewellery is to enhance and beautify fashionable women, such choices of imagery might seem odd. It certainly seems that there was a demand for jewellery with a hint of erotic danger and exoticism.'[1]

Art Nouveau jewellery was also a site for experimentation with exotic cultures from the Near East, the Americas and the European past. A corsage ornament created in 1902 by René Lalique (1860–1945) embodies this tension between fine workmanship in sumptuous materials and threatening motifs. The ornament is composed of a dragonfly enlarged to 30 cm long, with a sphinx-like female bust (pl.31).[2]

JEWELLERY AS AN ART FORM

—

Due to the cost of its raw materials and the technical skills required for its production, jewellery has often been seen as the most elevated of the decorative

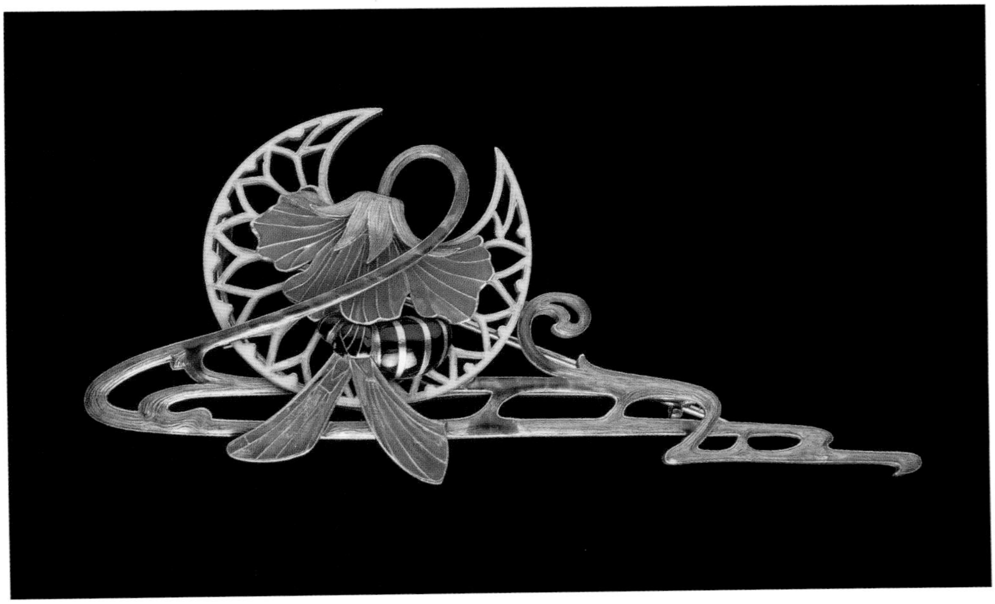

27 *opposite*
Lucien Gautrait, peacock pendant
Gold, enamel, diamonds, opals, emeralds
France, *c.*1900
V&A: 965–1901

28 *right*
Charles Desrosiers (designer) and Georges Fouquet (maker), brooch with flower and hornet
Gold and enamel
Paris, 1901
V&A: M.116–1966

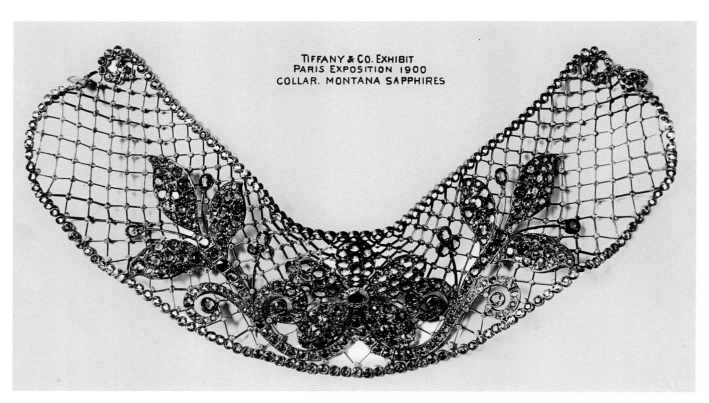

TIFFANY & CO. EXHIBIT
PARIS EXPOSITION 1900
COLLAR. MONTANA SAPPHIRES

arts. This link was confirmed by the work of the artist Alphonse Mucha (1860–1939), who first designed items of jewellery for the Parisian retailer Georges Fouquet (1862–1957), and then the boutique in which to sell them (pls 30 and 32).[3] This luxurious space was dedicated to female beauty, with nude women draped in jewels on the façade and in the stained glass windows, and a large peacock on the wall behind the counter. Mucha and Fouquet also collaborated in 1899 on a special commission for Sarah Bernhardt (1844–1923), creating a serpent bracelet that referred to her stage roles as *Medea* and *Cleopatra* (see pl.93).[4] Yet Fouquet also designed mass-produced pieces for more modest customers, such as an enamelled brooch that combines a naturalistic flower and insect with an abstract shape that references both an Islamic crescent, an Egyptian lotus blossom and an undulating wave form derived from Japanese woodblock prints (pl.28). This mixture of cultural and aesthetic references exemplifies the varied roots of Art Nouveau decorative arts, which built on earlier interest in exotic art forms.

The jewellers Tiffany and Co. had been actively collecting Japanese and Native American art since the 1870s, even exhibiting silver copies of Zuni baskets in Paris in 1900.[5] Louis Comfort Tiffany (1848–1933), son of the firm's founder, benefited from this breadth of references and from personal study trips to Europe and the Near East. His own design practice spanned architecture; domestic and ecclesiastical interiors; stained glass; lighting fixtures; decorative objects in glass, ceramic and enamelled metal; and finally

29 *opposite above*
Tiffany and Co., choker collar in gold and Montana sapphires
From *Photographs of the Tiffany & Co. Exhibit, Paris Exposition 1900*
London, 1900
V&A: NAL

30 *opposite left*
Alphonse Mucha, designs for jewellery
From *Documents décoratifs*
Paris, 1902

31 *opposite right*
René Lalique, dragonfly corsage ornament
Gold, chrysophase, moonstones, diamonds, enamel
Paris, 1897–8
Museu Calouste Gulbenkian, Lisbon

32 *right*
Alphonse Mucha, interior of Georges Fouquet's jewellery shop, Paris, 1903 (detail)
From *The Lady's Realm*, no.XV

jewellery. L.C. Tiffany's approach to jewellery design was quite different from
that of the family firm, which even at its most innovative – the lacework collars
shown in Paris in 1900, for example – relied on precious metals and gemstones
for their effect (pl.29).

L.C. Tiffany's first commercial jewellery designs were shown at the St Louis
Louisiana Purchase Exposition in 1904 and included insects, wild flowers and
fruits rendered in enamelled metal accented with semi-precious stones.[6] This
choice of subject matter aligned Tiffany with the avant-garde designs being
produced in France by Lucien Gaillard (1862–1933) and René Lalique, although
Tiffany's pieces were more brightly coloured than their work in glass and horn.
Like Lalique, Tiffany's jewellery was aligned to his work in other media,
particularly after he took over the jewellery division of Tiffany & Co. in 1907,
so that the wearer became a walking work of art.[7]

The stand of René Lalique at the Exposition Universelle 1900 was a triumph
of design, with a bronze grille formed of nude butterfly-women whose openwork
wings were backed with gauze that formed a display surface for his wares.[8]
It demonstrated the jeweller's mastery of materials, combining translucent
and opaque, rigid and flexible, matte and reflective in a similar way to his
ornaments. These show an acute observation of natural forms, both noble
and base – wayside weeds and insects were common subjects, as in the work
of other Art Nouveau jewellers such as Gaillard (pl.33).

33
**Lucien Gaillard,
hawthorn parasol handle,
owned by Heather Firbank**
Horn, pearls, rubies
Paris, c.1900
V&A: M.5:1–1980

This openness to subjects previously considered beneath notice was undoubtedly influenced by Japanese art, particularly by *netsuke*, which replicated insects, sea creatures and plants in minute detail (pl.34). These miniature sculptures had become popular with European connoisseurs by 1900, joining Japanese woodblock prints, ceramics and metalwork as collectable items. Lalique pieces such as his iris belt buckle make direct reference to Japanese *tsuba* (sword guards), iron plaques pierced with openwork designs of plants and family crests (pl.35). Lalique even adapted Japanese lacquer patterns for the leather gift boxes containing some of his pieces.[9]

What set Lalique's work apart from his contemporaries' was his understanding of sculptural form; fully rounded motifs set against low-relief backgrounds relieved by openwork piercing gave each piece an unprecedented depth and liveliness. He was a master in the use of translucent or openwork elements that allowed the colour of the hair or the dress they rested on to show through, thus accommodating themselves to each wearer (pl.36). Another factor in his success was his work at different levels of the market, which included opening a boutique selling glass flasks and vases in 1905, and designing moulded perfume bottles for the manufacturer Coty from 1908.[10]

PRECIOUS DESIGN, NOT PRECIOUS MATERIALS

From 1890 to 1914 there was an increased emphasis on the role of design over that of materials, with jewellery made from glass and horn, and fine artists designing paper fans. As accessories and jewellery became more closely linked to the fashion system, the ability to keep up with the latest in design became a mark of status, even when the cost of the individual items was less than that of traditional heirloom pieces.[11] Moreover, technical innovations in materials such as enamel and glass produced aesthetic effects that were attractive and novel, and in sympathy with trends in interior decoration. The perfecting of '*plique à jour*' (enamel made without a backing plate) led to a revival of enamel jewellery, no longer used as a cheap substitute for gem settings but embraced for its translucency and iridescent colour. Jewels such as an orchid hair ornament by Philippe Wolfers (1858–1929) united this technique with close observation of natural forms to create an object that surpasses nature (pl.37).

The use of semi-precious or non-precious materials in Art Nouveau designs made such jewellery and accessories available to the mass-market. From 1899, Liberty & Co. offered a range of 'Cymric' silver and enamel goods for the home and for personal ornament, many designed by Archibald Knox (1864–1933) to incorporate references to Celtic art.[12] These pieces appeared hand-worked, but were made using casting and stamping techniques which brought the price of a brooch down to 5s 6d, less than a tenth of the price of some Liberty garments (see pl.101).[13] By 1906, the French journalist Camille Mauclair lamented the ubiquity of Art Nouveau accessories: 'even the smallest haberdasher sells "modern style" hatpins for twenty sous'.[14]

34 *above*
Cicada toggle (*netsuke*)
Carved wood
Japan, *c.*1800–75
V&A: A.993-1910

35 *left*
Sword guard (*tsuba*)
Iron with gold and
silver inlay
Japan, 1700–1800
V&A: M.68-1920
**René Lalique, iris belt
buckle**
Partially gilt silver
Paris, *c.*1895
V&A: M.111-1966

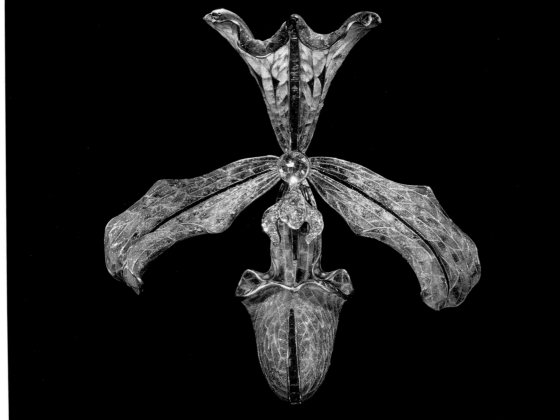

36 *above*
René Lalique, haircomb
Horn, pressed glass, topaz
Paris, 1903
V&A: M.116–1966

37 *right*
**Philippe Wolfers, orchid
hair ornament**
Gold, translucent enamel,
diamonds, rubies
Belgium, *c.*1906
V&A: M11–1962

ACCESSORIES

After jewellery, fans were traditionally the most precious female accessories, with guards of ivory, tortoiseshell or mother-of-pearl set with semi-precious stones unfolding to reveal leaves of lace, silk or hand-painted paper. Duvelleroy, established in Paris in 1827 but with a branch in London, was the best-known fan manufacturer, providing examples in the latest shapes and colours to match contemporary fashions and repairing valuable antiques. Major couture houses also sold fans or fan leaves made by specialist craftsmen; Worth commissioned a hand-made black lace fan with a design of irises as part of the 1899 trousseau for Viscountess Harcourt (see pl.74).

Around 1900, there was an increased interest in the artistic possibilities of fans, and fine artists provided one-off watercolours or limited-edition prints composed to suit the restricted size and shape of the fan leaf. The art critic Aymer Vallance commented in 1902 that 'the scope for decoration that fans

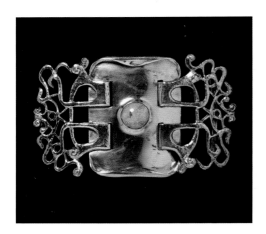 

afford is so great, and the possible methods so manifold, that the wonder is there are not many more artists employed in this industry'.[15] In 1911 Paquin commissioned the artists Paul Iribe (1883–1935), Georges Lepape (1887–1971) and Georges Barbier (1882–1932) to create designs for fans and fur accessories that were published in an illustrated album, *L'Éventail et la fourrure chez Paquin* (Paris, 1911); some of these were put into production, signed by both the artist and the couture house (pl.40).[16] Fans with printed or stencilled paper leaves representing scenes from fashionable life were widely used for advertising in France, where there were commercial artists who specialized in this area.[17]

For followers of fashion, seasonal changes in the shape, colour and texture of main garments required the renewing of accessories to match – not least the underwear that created the fashionable shape (see Chapter 5). Footwear was also important in producing the correct stance and style of movement, but until 1910 it was almost invisible under long skirts. However, the new 'hobble' skirts and *jupes culottes* focused the attention on the gait; evening dresses were wrapped

38 above left
'Cymric' belt buckle, probably designed by Oliver Baker and made by Haseler & Co., Birmingham, for Liberty & Co., 1899
Silver, opal
V&A: M.306-1975

39 above right
Alan McAfee, purple suede shoes, worn by Heather Firbank
London, 1910–14
V&A: T.149-1960
Hook, Knowles & Co., red kid shoes
London, c.1900
V&A: T.246-1979

or tucked up at the front to allow for dancing, and tailored suits were so narrow that side slits were needed for walking, revealing the wearer's feet and ankles to an extent not seen in decades. Denise Poiret accessorized her husband's ankle-skimming designs with flat boots in coloured leather for day, and pumps or Turkish-style slippers for evening.[18] Brightly coloured shoes like those worn by Heather Firbank (pl.39) emphasized the newly revealed feet; they also expressed the wearer's commitment to fashion, as different ensembles would require appropriately coloured footwear. At this time the most exclusive shoemaker in the world was Pietro Yantorny (1874–1936), a museum curator who made bespoke footwear from antique brocade and embroidery, stored on shoe trees made from dismantled violins in trunks lined with white velvet.[19]

Hats had always been an important part of the fashionable ensemble, as they complemented the overall silhouette of the garment and framed or shaded the wearer's face. Some kind of head covering was normal for women, men and children, outdoors and in public spaces such as restaurants and theatres. Even at home, lace caps were worn to cover hair that had not yet been styled for the day, and evening headdresses put the finishing touch to formal coiffures. For outdoor wear, hats were chosen to reflect the ensemble with which they were worn, though they were not always made to match; millinery was a separate profession, creating sculptural shapes from different varieties and textures of plaited straw, horsehair and moulded felt. As millinery did not require fitting to the body, it was an easier profession to enter than dressmaking; Gabrielle 'Coco' Chanel (1883–1971) had trained as a dressmaker, but she began her independent career when a wealthy lover set her up as a milliner in 1909.[20]

40
**Georges Barbier
for Paquin, fan**
Hand-coloured print on
paper, painted bone sticks
Paris, 1911
V&A: T.333–1978

Fashionable hats often incorporated exotic feathers (or even entire birds), artificial flowers and swathes of fabric, all of which were liable to damage by adverse weather, requiring frequent replacement. The size of women's headgear varied with fashion: in the early 1890s the vertical silhouette was reflected in small-brimmed hats with tall crowns; as the fashionable line shifted in 1895 to accentuate the breadth of the upper torso, coiffures were bulked out with hair extensions, pads and wire frames to support broad-brimmed hats held in place by hatpins up to 30 cm long. When narrow-skirted fashions were introduced they were offset by hats that were larger than ever, creating a columnar silhouette. This style was particularly linked with the costumes designed by Lucile for *The Merry Widow* in 1907 (see pl.47). These outsized hats were closely linked with the play, being given away to audience members at a gala performance in New York.[21] In complete contrast, evening headdresses at this time were close-fitting and exotic, modelled on Greek bandeaux, Indian turbans or Native American war bonnets. These shapes gradually filtered through to daytime use, and by 1913 smart walking ensembles were being accessorized with brimless toques decorated with a single vertical plume or aigrette.

The final detail for fashionable outdoor ensembles was the parasol or umbrella; parasol handles made by esteemed jewellers such as Fabergé or Gaillard were miniature works of art (pl.33).[22] Luxurious parasol frames like these might be re-covered at the end of the season to replace sun-damaged fabric or to suit a changing wardrobe. There were also fashions in the shapes of parasols themselves, from flat platters to pointed pagodas, and from round to octagonal or scalloped hems.

A new form of designer fashion accessory was inaugurated in 1911 when Poiret launched a range of perfume, 'Les parfums de Rosine'. Building on Coty's use of Lalique-designed flasks, Poiret gave each scent a particular theme that was carried through packaging and advertising: 'Minaret' came in a box shaped like a minaret and decorated with Arabic script, while 'Aladin' referenced Chinese carvings and Persian miniatures. These collectable flasks helped to consolidate the Poiret brand, and extended it to consumers unable to purchase the designer's more outré garments.[23]

Around 1900, the complexity of fashionable clothing meant that outer garments were essentially unwashable; even 'lingerie' dresses and blouses worn in summer were not meant to be washed frequently. Hygiene was maintained by layers of washable undergarments, and by adding washable collars and cuffs to non-washable dresses (see Chapter 5). These washable accessories also provided an opportunity to vary the ensemble, particularly for the cost-conscious consumer with a limited wardrobe. The most exclusive white accessories were in hand-made lace, more delicate than the silk dresses with which they were worn. Workshops in France, Belgium and Italy were still producing high-quality lace, including orders specially designed for clients such as Viscountess Harcourt (see pls 72–4). Alternatively, fashionable women could demonstrate their taste by wearing antique lace; the Callot sisters

41

Lace fan made in the Imperial Royal Central Lace-Course in Vienna, shown at the Louisiana Purchase Exposition, St Louis, 1904
From *Exhibition of Professional Schools for Arts and Crafts*
Vienna, 1904
V&A: NAL

specialized in reworking valuable antique Venetian needle lace into purses, collars and stoles (see Chapter 4). There were also initiatives to revive lace design to incorporate more modern motifs and styles of representation, with artist-led workshops set up in areas from Hungary to Honiton in Devon (pl.41).[24]

Art Nouveau fashion accessories embody a paradox; they are often highly prized by museums, frequently exhibited and published. Yet they are most often seen in isolation, with jewellery and fans displayed as self-sufficient artworks, rather than as elements of an ensemble. This is a contradiction of the Art Nouveau aesthetic, which valued the total effect over any individual part. In this sense, the use in jewellery of low-key materials such as translucent enamel and moulded horn can be seen as stepping back from the more overt appeal of precious metals and gemstones. However, the choice of subjects such as insects, reptiles and weeds made these jewels attention-catching. New fashions in shoes were equally distinctive, drawing the viewer's eye to an area of the body that had previously been decently obscure, while fashionable hats were so large that they dominated social spaces. Altogether, fashion accessories allowed the wearer to demonstrate her taste, her modernity, and her disregard for conventions, while being impeccably dressed.

CHAPTER 3

PROMOTING FASHION

—

By 1890, information about fashion was more widely available than ever before, in print media, in advertising images and through stage shows (soon to be followed by films). Improvements in print technology meant that fashion illustrations – engraved, lithographed or photographed – could be included in even the cheapest publications, or distributed in formats ranging from small leaflets to billboard-sized posters.

FASHION PUBLICATIONS

—

Illustrated fashion magazines were well established by 1890; improvements in print technology, in cheap wood-based paper stock and in mail distribution networks had created the ideal conditions for a boom in periodicals.[1] In these publications fashion was discussed at different levels: coloured fashion plates showed a vision of the new fashion (not necessarily based on extant garments), as in the highly decorated 'hobble' skirts drawn for *The Gentlewoman* in 1914 (pl.42), while fashion columns gave accounts of what was worn by the social elite, even when this was not appropriate for the lives of the readers.

There were also publications that included technical information on new styles. Some, like *The Ladies' Tailor* (London) (pl.44), sold only to professionals who were able to draft their own patterns from technical diagrams. Other publications, such as *Le Moniteur de la Mode* (Paris) or *The Queen* (London),

42 *opposite*
Jules de Ban, fashion drawing for *The Gentlewoman*
Watercolour, 54 x 39.5 cm
Paris or London, 1914
V&A: E.2945-1962

43 *right*
Embroidery pattern sheet
From *Paris Journal of Fancy Work and Fashion*, London, November 1910
56 x 89 cm
V&A: E.194-2010

offered pattern sheets that could be adapted for use by competent amateurs. There were also magazines from which readers could order tissue patterns cut to size; these were sometimes published by dressmaking pattern companies, as with Butterick's *Delineator* (New York) and *Myra's Journal* (London).[2]

In industrial nations like Britain, the growing number of women employed in teaching and other professions increased the pool of consumers for low-cost fashion; they were served by numerous magazines giving practical advice and instructions, such as *Mrs Schild's Penny Dressmaker* (pl.43).[3] There were also fashion features in nearly all general publications; even *Votes for Women*, journal of the militant Women's Social and Political Union, had a column advising readers how they could shop while supporting the Suffragette cause.[4]

The growth of mass-market fashion magazines led to differentiation between publications: *Les Modes* (Paris, 1901) and *Vogue* (New York, 1892) promoted the work of the leading couturiers with large, glossy photographs of house models, of exhibitions in the magazine's offices, and of society ladies.[5] The *Gazette du bon ton* (Paris, 1912) (pl.51) and *Journal des dames et des modes* (Paris, revived 1912) returned to the small formats and hand-coloured engravings of early nineteenth-century publications to promote avant-garde designs by Poiret and others (see Chapter 7). The *Gazette* gave the illustrators involved – all of whom were recognized as artists – an unprecedented degree of freedom in design, and a share in the profits.[6] Meanwhile *Comoedia illustré* (Paris), *Play Pictorial* (London) and *The Theater* (New York) presented the clothes worn by actresses and dancers both on and off the stage.[7]

FASHION DISPLAYS IN STORES

During the 1890s, retailers' methods of promoting fashion became increasingly sophisticated. Marketing leaflets and mail-order catalogues illustrated with line engravings had been used since the 1840s, as had fashion publications with detailed drawings and pattern diagrams of the latest styles for men, women and children.[8] Improved printing methods encouraged the production of large publicity posters, first in black and white and then in full-colour lithography.[9] These were displayed in retailers' windows, on buses and on advertising hoardings, making fashion information more widely available than ever before (pl.45).

Retailers had installed large plate glass windows from the 1860s, but these had often been used to present a visual catalogue of everything the store had to offer, overwhelming the shopper. From the 1880s a more considered approach resulted in window displays with fewer and more carefully co-ordinated items, changed regularly to reflect seasonal events or fashions.[10] Frequent changes also lessened the damage caused to the goods displayed by sunlight, dust and fumes from gas lamps. The spread of electricity from the 1880s permitted brighter and cleaner lighting for shop windows and interiors.

"Ladies' Tailor" Fashions

January, 1899

Entered at Stationer's Hall.

Published by The John Williamson Company, Limited. London, W.C.

44
Fashion plate
From *The Ladies' Tailor*,
London, January 1899
V&A: E.1602–1946

Advances in shop display and promotional practices were often seen as deriving from the United States, an association drawn on by the American entrepreneur Gordon Selfridge when he established his London store in 1909 with novel features such as a passenger elevator.[11] However, Selfridge was not alone in his attention to presentation, which could involve considerable expense for retailers. A 1911 catalogue from a specialist shopfitter in Birmingham included figures for displaying three current skirt shapes: flared, straight or 'hobble', and the 'harem or ankle skirt', costing up to £9. It also offered electrically powered display fittings such as rotating stands and illuminated leg forms to show off fine silk stockings.[12] The 1913 Ghent International Exhibition had a separate category for fashion display; one of the firms that participated was producing 30,000 figures a year.[13]

FASHION ONSTAGE

The stage spectacle, which allowed the audience to view costumes for hours at a time, and to revisit them in illustrated newspapers and souvenir photographs of the stars, was an essential tool of fashion promotion around 1900. Actresses were especially important in launching new fashions in Paris, New York and London through drawing-room comedies or the genre of plays set in department stores.[14] Garments seen onstage and in the audience were detailed in fashion journals and press reports, and designers were happy to supply leading ladies at a discount in return for acknowledgement in the programme.[15] In 1908, the couturier Redfern placed an advertisement informing clients that they could see his latest designs onstage in three different plays, as well as at the Franco-British exhibition and in his London and Paris showrooms (pl.46).[16] Some actresses were dressed by the same designers both offstage and on; after the success of Lucile's costumes for *The Merry Widow* (1907), the lead actress Lily Elsie dressed exclusively in Lucile, becoming a walking advertisement (pl.47).[17] Others used their reputation as fashion innovators to launch products in their own names; Jane Hading, a rival of Sarah Bernhardt, launched the 'Eau de Jeunesse Jane Hading' beauty preparation in 1909.[18]

The extent to which the theatre played a role in fashion publicity was revealed by journalists' reactions when directors dressed actresses in character rather than for display. The impecunious Nora in Ibsen's *A Doll's House* (1889) was criticized as dowdy, while the flower-seller-turned-lady Eliza Doolittle in Shaw's *Pygmalion* (1913) was seen as distressingly vulgar.[19] Equally controversial were theatrical spectacles presenting styles that were too extreme for everyday wear, but which nevertheless changed the direction of fashion. In 1910 Jeanne Paquin designed costumes for the actress Cora Lapercerie in *Xantho chez les courtisanes*, written by Lapercerie's husband Jacques Richepin. For this comedy set in Ancient Greece, Paquin reinterpreted classical 'chitons' with drapery pulled tight around the body. These designs both showed off the leading lady's figure and presented an exaggeration of the fashionable narrow silhouette.[20]

45
Advertising showcard for 'Hixopad' heel tips
Colour lithography on card,
30 x 20 cm
London, 1911
National Archives, Kew

In 1912 Paquin made up the costumes for *Rue de la Paix*, a comedy set in rival fashion salons, one of which produced garments in conventional good taste, and the other 'the decors of the harem'.[21] The costumes designed by Paul Iribe, one of Poiret's favoured illustrators, promoted ensembles similar to those offered by

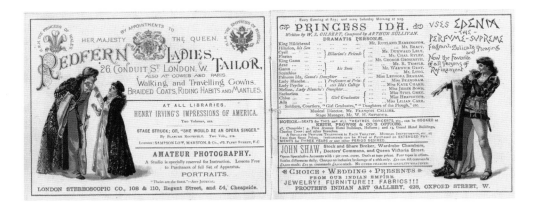

Paquin and mocked the exotic styles associated with Poiret.[22] These projects allowed Paquin to demonstrate her awareness of the latest orientalist styles, while maintaining a critical distance from them.

In 1913 Poiret responded to these challenges with his designs for *Le Minaret*, another vehicle written by Richepin for Lapercerie. This was set in a Middle-Eastern fantasy land and its actresses were dressed in Turkish-style trousers, sheer tunics with wired hems, and uncorseted bodices. Poiret had been promoting a version of these styles since his 1911 '1002nd Night' party, where guests were required to don orientalist costumes (see pl.10).[23] However, the 1913 designs pushed the limits of decency; Denise Poiret's ensemble for the opening of *Le Minaret* had sheer pantaloons through which brief satin undershorts were clearly visible.[24] These costumes were satirized in the book of French cartoons *Le Vrai et le faux chic*, and in the Keystone comedy film *Tillie's Punctured Romance*.[25] The '*jupes culottes*' with which Poiret was associated were also satirized in the London music-hall revue *Keep Smiling* (pl.48). However, the orientalist costumes presented onstage not only brought Poiret's name before the public, they also highlighted the refreshing simplicity of the tunic dresses he was producing for sale (see pl.19).

FASHION ALBUMS, PHOTOGRAPHS AND FILMS

In addition to their work for the stage, fashion houses presented their main seasonal collections directly to clients through a variety of pictorial media. Albums of fashion drawings, hand-painted in gouache with meticulous detailing, were compiled by Paquin and Lucile (see pls 7 and 16). Several identical copies were made for distribution to branches of the main house, or for loan to clients and journalists. The danger of designs being copied for illicit

46
Redfern advertisement in the programme for *Princess Ida*
Savoy Theatre, London, 1884

47
Lily Elsie in costume
designed by Lucile for
The Merry Widow, 1907

reproduction was dealt with by imposing a strict time limit for loans and a fee for non-return. The Lucile drawings had samples of the fabrics and trimmings for each design attached to the edge of the page, making it easier for clients to envisage the effect of the finished garment, and to negotiate any alterations (see pl.17).[26]

The House of Worth took a different approach, compiling black-and-white photograph albums for each season's collection. The images were functional, with the garments placed on dressmaking stands, a mirror to show the back view and a panel giving the reference number for the style. These photographs would help to protect against copyists, and could also be shown to clients. For an international business like Worth, photographs had the advantage over sketches in that they were easier to duplicate for different branches.

Since the 1860s, photographs printed on card had been the accepted method of recording an individual's appearance, both for personal use and for publicity purposes. Photographers engaged to take portraits of celebrities often retained the right of reproduction, so that images of royalty, actors and other notables were widely displayed and sold.[27] A change in postal regulations opened the way for pictorial postcards of actors or society beauties dressed in the latest fashions.[28]

Fashion photography for fashion magazines started to be used during the 1890s, and *Les Modes* used photographs for all its illustrations, with full-page tinted plates in each issue. Fashion photography could not show construction lines in as much detail as an engraved drawing could; this might have been an advantage for designers who feared that published images would be copied by

48
Scene from *Keep Smiling* featuring Poiret's *'jupes culottes'*
Alhambra Theatre,
London, 1913

their rivals. Photographs could also create atmospheric images to draw in the viewer, as with Edward Steichen's photographs of Poiret garments published in an article in *Art et decoration* (1911) (pl.49).

The development of moving pictures opened up further possibilities for fashion promotion, with fashionable ensembles shown on moving bodies and projected at life-size. Early feature films continued the practices of the contemporary theatre, with actors providing their own costumes. However, by 1914 Hollywood producers had started to see fashion as a way of attracting audiences and additional revenue. Popular serials such as *The Perils of Pauline* featured up-to-the-minute ensembles by leading designers, including Lucile and Poiret. These styles were then written up in newspaper fashion features, providing valuable cross-promotion.[29] By 1913 newsreels of fashion shows from Paris and London included the tinted *Kinemacolor Fashion Gazette*.[30] One London journalist commented: 'Of all stages, that of the cinema theatre is the most concentrated, the most tumultuous, and, in a sense, the most convincing.'[31]

FASHION SHOWS IN SALONS AND FASHION PROMOTION

The presentation of fashion shows in stage and film spectacles revealed the increasing importance given to presenting garments within the fashion industry. This was particularly important for couture houses, which relied on orders from individual clients seeking exclusive garments not on display to the general public. In the 1860s Charles Frederick Worth had used his wife as a publicity agent, taking her out to society events dressed in his latest fashions. From 1900 Madame Paquin, in addition to appearing at society events herself, sent house models or actresses dressed in her designs to race meetings, where they were photographed by fashion magazines like *Les Modes*.[32]

By the 1890s, all couture houses had developed a range of in-house and external publicity strategies to attract and increase sales. One was to present the showroom as a site of leisure, with clients calling in regularly to meet friends and check on new styles. This is exemplified by Henri Gervex's painting *Cinq heures chez Paquin*, exhibited at the Salon of 1906, in which fashionable ladies socialize while being shown fabric samples or model garments by white-bloused 'vendeuses' (pl.50). Even more effective were displays of garments on live models circulating among the clients so garments could be seen close up.[33] Around 1913 Paquin and other couturiers presented tea dances, which allowed the clients to see how appropriate the styles were for new, energetic dances like the tango.[34]

The next innovation was to present fashion shows as staged spectacles (pl.52). Although the couturier Lucile claimed to have originated fashion parades in 1904, she was building on earlier practice in department stores and at international exhibitions. However, Lucile's salon shows were more carefully presented than her rivals', with music and lighting used to enhance the effect of her 'gowns of emotion'.[35] The presence of clients' husbands viewing model girls in revealing clothes raised concerns for contemporaries: 'they were invited to

49
**Edward Steichen, colour
photograph of Poiret's
'Enfer' dress**
From *Art et decoration*,
Paris, April 1911

50
**Henri Gervex
(1852–1929), *Cinq heures
chez Paquin***
Oil on canvas, 300 x 172 cm
Paris, 1906
House of Worth, London

stare and smile, and they did. But there was something remarkably offensive in their way of doing it' (pl.51).[36] This concern was based on long-standing debates about the exploitation of young women in the garment industry by male employers and clients. However, by giving her mannequins exotic names such as 'Gamela' and 'Sumurun', and presenting them as 'personalities', Lucile created the role of the fashion model as an independent woman. Some of them went on to become showgirls or to marry into the social elite.[37]

EXHIBITIONS AND INTERNATIONAL AUDIENCES

Another form of fashion promotion that became more important after 1900 was display at international exhibitions. Clothing had, of course, been displayed from the 1851 London Great Exhibition onwards; there had even been an entire event devoted to dress at the International Health Exhibitions in London in 1883 and 1884.[38] Exhibition medals awarded for the best items in specific classes – shoes, corsets, knitted underwear, dress trimmings, fans – were proudly reproduced in publicity material for decades afterwards. International exhibitions attracted people with many different dress practices, and provided ideal opportunities for observing or showing off new styles, including controversial ones. At the World's Columbian Exposition in Chicago in 1893, a congress debated proposals to 'reform' dress in the interests of health, and the

LE CHOIX DIFFICILE

Manteau du soir de Worth

outfits worn by delegates (including shortened skirts and full 'Turkish' trousers) attracted a great deal of attention.[39] There was also a pageant of national costumes on live models presented by the International Dress and Costume Company.[40] Categories for garments and fashion accessories – including hairstyling – were included in the Manufactures Building. However, the much-vaunted Women's Building did not include any fashion displays – other than on the bodies of its committee, headed by Mrs Potter Palmer (see Chapter 4).

It was at the Exposition Universelle 1900 that fashion became a major attraction, both as a form of entertainment and as a reflection of the commercial importance of the clothing trade. The tone was set by the ceremonial arch at the entrance to the Exposition, topped with a giant statue representing 'La Parisienne' in fashionable clothing designed by Jeanne Paquin.[41] Inside there was a 'Palais du Costume', containing 34 tableaux designed by the couturier Félix and the stage designer Thomas, with accurately dressed and staged waxwork figures showing the development of fashion from Ancient Egypt to 1900. This provided a pedigree for the luxurious garments presented in the next section by the trade body of Paris couture, the 'Collectivité de la Couture', in large vitrines sponsored by different firms. Worth showed a lady dressing for presentation at the Court of St James in London, while Paquin's display had a figure with a portrait head of Madame Paquin seated at a dressing table decked with the silver toilette set of the lady herself.[42] There were also smaller cases with individual ensembles that could be inspected at close quarters both by fashion professionals and by curious visitors who would rarely have a chance to see court presentation gowns such as the one exhibited by the Callot sisters, with its sequinned lace drapery, three-dimensional silk flowers, and toning satin train (pl.56). Some of

51 *opposite*
**Bernard Boutet de Monvel,
'Le Choix difficile,
manteau du soir de Worth'**
From *Gazette du bon ton*,
April 1914, plate 40

52 *above*
**Fashion show in the Salon
of Lucile Ltd, Paris, c.1910**
V&A: AAD/2008/6/28

the garments were updated weekly to show the very latest styles, with a live fashion show that became a 'society rendezvous'.[43] The Collectivité de la Couture published a lavishly illustrated souvenir album with hand-tinted plates and detailed descriptions of the main ensembles displayed. The survival of sketches of some of the Paquin garments exhibited in 1900 allows us to compare the designer's visualization with its final realization. For a red day ensemble, the train on the skirt was reduced and the cuffs adjusted to create a bracelet-like wristband (pls 53 and 54).

The importance of the Palais du Costume as a visitor attraction was acknowledged when the historic tableaux were reinstalled at the Paris in London Exhibition in Earl's Court in 1902, with some contemporary ensembles from 1902, but apparently without the couture section.[44] At the 1904 Louisiana Purchase Exhibition held in St Louis there was a display of fashion from forty-four firms, including some department stores, and separate installations from Paquin, Redfern and others, as well as a number of the historical tableaux.[45] In addition, artist-designed textiles and fashion accessories in Secessionist style were exhibited in the Austrian pavilion (see Chapter 7).[46]

Fashion was very much at the centre of the Franco-British Exhibition staged in London in 1908, as an attraction and as a representation of French skills in the design and production of luxury goods. As in 1900, the fashion section was organized by the Collectivité de la Couture – including the recently established Paul Poiret. Reviewers found some designs unwearable: 'exaggerated Directoire and Incroyable gowns, with their eel-tight clinging to the figure, their skin-tight sleeves and long, narrow pointed trains'.[47] However, they approved of the brilliant effect produced by the electric lighting, still a novelty (the electricity

Robe de ville taffetas framboise
Modèle de Paquin

53 *far left*
Paquin, day ensemble
From *Les Toilettes de la collectivité de la Couture, Exposition universelle internationale de 1900*
Paris, 1900
V&A: NAL

54 *left*
Paquin, design for day ensemble shown at the Exposition Universelle 1900, Paris
From album for 'Été 1900'
Pencil with gouache
V&A: E341–1957

supply in the Exposition Universelle 1900 was erratic): 'the embroideries, many of which are of gold or jewels, flash and sparkle and reflect the light in such a manner that they exhibit to the full the idea of the designer.'[48] There was also great interest in the displays by specialists in corsets, lingerie, perfume and furs. The furrier Revillon presented tableaux showing stages of the fur trade, while their rivals Grunwaldt recreated their luxury boutique with Louis XIV style décor (pl.58).[49]

By the 1911 Turin International Exhibition, the historic tableaux seem to have been retired, but French couturiers still staged a two-part exhibition. The main section was a display (pl.55) by representatives of French couture (not including Poiret) and alongside it was a smaller pavilion devoted to the work of Paquin.[50] This had a classical theme, with posed figures and painted friezes of scantily clad Greek nymphs based on Paquin's designs for *Xantho chez les courtisanes*, contrasting with her more decorous designs for actual wear.

Thus between 1890 and 1914 international couturiers embraced a range of strategies to promote their designs – and their reputation for innovation. Displays at major exhibitions reinforced designers' reputations as international fashion leaders. Publishing drawings and photographs in illustrated magazines promoted seasonal design innovations; however, it also meant that these innovations would be swiftly adopted by rivals – as with the 1900 fashion for irregular, coralline shapes, originated by Worth and soon taken up by smaller houses (pl.57). Dressing stars of stage and screen increased column inches in

Robe de Cour

Callot sœurs

56
Callot Soeurs, court dress
From *Les Toilettes de la
collectivité de la Couture,
Exposition universelle
internationale de 1900*
Paris, 1900
V&A: NAL

newspapers, on both society and fashion pages, while hosting events such as tea parties and model parades gave potential clients the opportunity to see the latest styles close up on moving bodies. If these initiatives made designers' work too familiar, albums of drawings and swatches could be used to create something exclusive for the client.

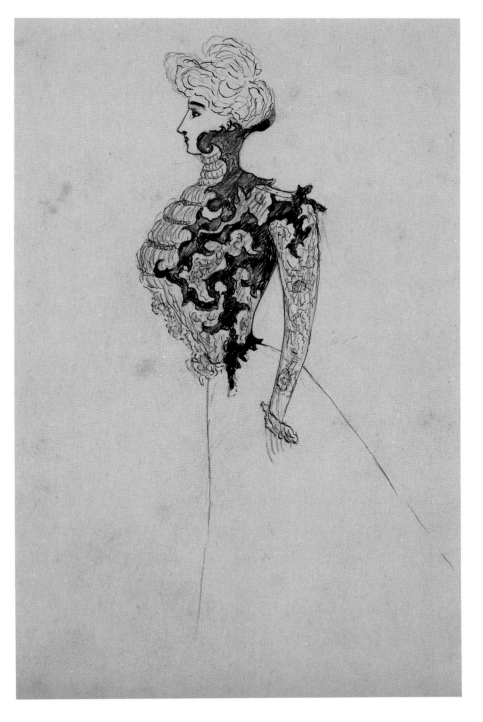

57
Maison Arnold, bodice design
Pencil drawing from album
Paris, c.1900
V&A: AAD/1984/5

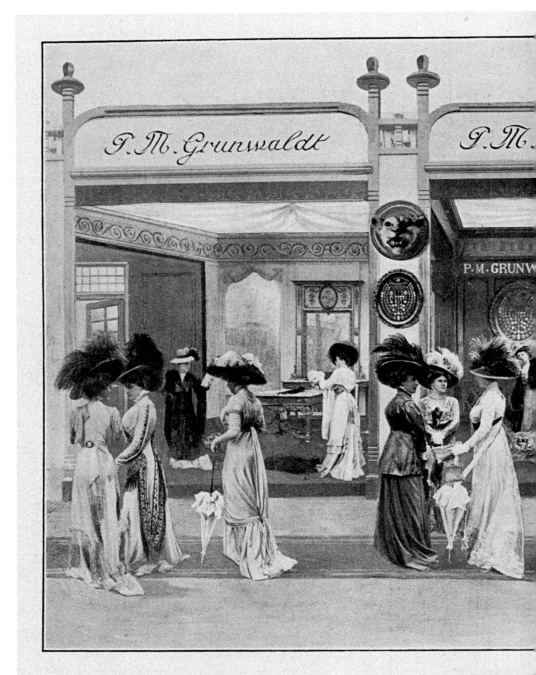

58
P.M. Grunwaldt,
fur exhibit
From *The Franco British*
Exhibition illustrated
review
London, 1908

M. GRUNWALDT'S EXHIBIT.

CHAPTER 4
FASHION PATRONS

—

Maintaining good relationships with clients was one of the most challenging aspects of running a couture house. One factor that caused problems was lack of agreement over pricing, since garments rarely had a set price. Even when a price had been agreed, changes to fabric, trimming or cut during the process of commissioning could add considerably to the cost. Bills were normally presented a month, or even three months, after purchase, by which time the client's memory as to what she had agreed might have faded.[1] In this light, couturiers' self-description as 'artists' made good commercial sense, as clients might be reluctant to haggle with an 'artist'.

A further complication was the legal status of married women; minors under the law, they could not be sued for non-payment, and if the couturier sued the husband he might deny any knowledge of the commission and refuse to pay. Inviting husbands to accompany their wives to garment showings and fittings was one way to avoid this problem.[2] If all else failed, a client might be blacklisted for non-payment; in 1885 the main couture houses created a common blacklist, which created a scandal when it was leaked to the press.[3]

The patrons of Art Nouveau high fashion fell into several distinct categories. In the first were the women whose social status (based on aristocratic lineage, inherited wealth, or marriage) required an elaborate wardrobe for high-profile public appearances. Often neither young nor adventurous in their tastes, they tended to patronize established couture houses, principally Worth. The House of Worth kept detailed notes of the physical requirements, engagements and social circles of their principal clients, such as the Empress Marie Feodorovna of Russia and Princess Maud of Norway.[4] They knew the dress regulations at the major European courts, and how to design around the large-scale jewelled stars and orders worn by royalty for official functions. In general, the patronage of high-status clients provided publicity for the couture houses, and set a seal of social approval on their designs: 'the new creations . . . never really become fashionable . . . until after they have undergone those modifications by the great ladies, which are needed to deprive them of their pristine vulgarity and consequent lack of true chic and elegance'.[5]

Very different in their requirements were women who were in the public eye as actresses, singers or professional beauties. Their reputations rested on their ability to surprise the public with novel or distinctive fashions, and designers were happy to oblige them with loans or gifts of their latest styles. But perhaps most interesting was the third category of influential fashion patrons: women whose wealth enabled them to indulge a personal sense of style that was not limited by social conventions.

59
**Paul Nadar, Countess
Greffulhe in Worth
evening gown**
Paris, 1896
Réunion Musées
Nationaux de France

60
**Laferrière, evening dress,
worn by the Princess of
Wales, future Queen
Alexandra**
Figured silk satin and net,
imitation pearls
Paris, c.1900
V&A: T.282A-1974

PRINCESSES

The summit of the *fin-de-siècle* social hierarchy was represented by the crowned heads of Europe, notably the Queen Empress of England and the Empresses of Russia and Germany, who needed wardrobes to reflect their exalted status. From the 1870s onwards, illustrated newspapers and fashion journals were publishing detailed accounts of royal clothing, not only for state occasions such as coronations, jubilees and weddings, but also for private events such as country weekends. Photographs, engravings from sketches and verbal descriptions ensured that innovations would be noted, and any falling-off of standards commented on. Even the most elevated personages might quail before this level of public scrutiny and seek reassurance from fashion advisors. This was a role that Charles Frederick Worth was only too happy to fulfil, as he claimed in an 1895 interview:

> *Those ladies are the wisest who leave the choice to us ... For example, a telegram came from the Empress of Russia, 'Send me a dinner dress!' Nothing more. We are left absolute freedom as to style and material. Not that the Empress is indifferent in the matter of dress. Quite the contrary. She will sometimes require that all the ladies' costumes at a certain ball be pink, or red, or blue ... The point is she trusts our judgement rather than her own.*[6]

Empress Marie Feodorovna of Russia (originally Princess Dagmar of Denmark) was happy to rely on Worth over a thirty-year period; she commissioned the firm to supply matching outfits for herself and her sister, the future Queen Alexandra of England, to wear on family holidays in Denmark.[7] Alexandra herself patronized a number of French and British firms: French for evening gowns, and English for day dresses and tailoring.[8] The designer with whom she was most closely associated was John Redfern (1853–1929), originally a tailor located on the Isle of Wight near the royal summer residence. After being commissioned to provide leisure clothing for the Princess and her children to wear on seaside holidays, Redfern became acknowledged as a leader in ladies' and children's tailoring.[9] Alexandra seems to have had a taste for simplicity; an evening dress she commissioned from Laferrière of Paris is made from silk damask with matching tulle trim, its main impact coming from large artificial pearl drops at the neckline and waist (pl.60).

For the most significant event in her life, her 1902 coronation, Alexandra ordered two dresses from Worth, but the gown for the ceremony itself was made up by the smaller Paris house of Morin-Blossier at a cost of £996.[10] The fabric for the dress was commissioned in India by the Vicereine, Lady Mary Curzon.[11] The Indian embroidery depicted British national flowers in Indian techniques, producing a textile that embodied 'Empire'. Equally important for Alexandra, the dress of gold gauze over a cloth-of-gold foundation was unique to her, a distinction she insisted on in letters to Lady Curzon: 'The Queen wishes me to write and ask you not to tell anyone in *England* about the dresses ordered in India, or else they will be wanting to have some also, whereas H[er] M[ajesty] would like to have something *original* for her Coronation dress.'[12]

The possibility of gowns being duplicated, undermining the wearer's sartorial identity, was a real one, as was shown when in 1912 Alexandra's daughter, Queen Maud of Norway, and her niece, Queen Victoria Eugenia of Spain, both ordered versions of the same Worth evening dress, 'Arlésienne' (pls 64–6). Even if these dresses were not worn at the same event, press photographs of the royal wearers – both granddaughters of Queen Victoria of England – would have made the duplication evident.

Lady Mary Curzon, the Chicago-born wife of Lord Curzon, Viceroy of India from 1899 to 1905, took her own official wardrobe very seriously. She frequently commissioned Indian textiles, which were then made up by couture houses, including Worth – the most famous of these was the 'Peacock Gown' for the State Ball in Delhi to celebrate the 1902 coronation (pl.61).[13] Although Indian embroideries and brocades were much cheaper than European-made equivalents, Lady Curzon's clothing still outstripped her means and was subsidized by her father Levi Leiter, one of the founders of Marshall Field's department store in Chicago.[14]

61
**Albert Edward Jeakins,
Lady Curzon dressed
for the Delhi Durbar**
London, 1903
National Portrait Gallery,
London

62 *opposite left*
**Worth, evening dress,
worn by Mrs Potter
Palmer**
Satin, velvet, metallic
embroidery, beads,
artificial flowers
Paris, 1893
Chicago History Museum

63 *opposite right*
**Photograph of Mrs Potter
Palmer in an evening
gown by Worth**
Chicago, c.1894
Chicago History Museum

MERCHANT PRINCESSES

—

As the personal histories of Mary Leiter Curzon, Consuelo Vanderbilt Marlborough, and other 'Dollar Princesses' show, there were many links between the American mercantile elite and European aristocracy. Even without a formal title, however, there were many women who were accepted as leaders of society and of fashion on both sides of the Atlantic. Charles Frederick Worth saw them as his most important patrons, and in 1884 he was quoted as saying: 'American women are the best customers he has – far better than queens. *They* ask the price; American women never do. They simply say, "Give me the best, the most beautiful, the most fashionable gown."'[15]

American clients who visited Paris in order to renew their wardrobes were in the habit of settling their bills on delivery, making a refreshing contrast to European clients who dragged out payments over months or even years.[16] Worth's prices were high; in 1871 his principal clients spent between £400 and £4,000 each year with him, in addition to garments and accessories from other firms. This was at a time when £100 a year was a standard salary for middle-class professionals like school teachers.[17]

64 above
Worth, 'Arlésienne'
evening dress, worn by
Queen Maud of Norway
Silk and tulle, beaded
all over
Paris, 1912–13
National Museum of Art,
Architecture and Design,
Oslo

65 top
Worth, evening dress,
'Arlésienne', design
number 4332
Photograph from album,
Winter 1912–13
V&A: AAD/1/59/1982

66 bottom
Christian Franzen for
J. Beagles & Co.,
'Arlésienne' evening
dress, worn by Queen
Victoria Eugenia
of Spain
Postcard, 12.5 x 8 cm
London, 1912
National Portrait Gallery,
London

In the early 1890s, perhaps the most famous American woman in the world was Bertha Honoré (Mrs Potter) Palmer (1849–1918), who masterminded the construction and displays of the Woman's Building at the World's Columbian Exposition, Chicago, in 1893 (pl.63). This major project presented an 'object lesson in the history of woman's intellectual development, and . . . an unanswerable argument to those who have been wont to deny her ability to excel in any line of work outside that of light fancy work or household drudgery'.[18] It was supported by loans of exhibits from Queen Victoria of England, Queen Marguerite of Italy, and other members of the international elite, and from American organizations and individuals.

Mrs Palmer was possessed of formidable organizational abilities combined with personal wealth (her husband was the owner of an important department store and hotel) and impressive family connections (her sister had married the son of President Ulysses S. Grant).[19] Surviving garments in the collections of the Chicago History Museum indicate that her wardrobe was lavish and fashionable, but strictly conventional. For the opening of the Columbian Exposition she had an evening dress by Worth trimmed with silver embroidery and fur edging (pl.62). Her visit to the Exposition Universelle 1900 gave her the opportunity to commission evening gowns, street ensembles and negligees from the houses of Worth, Doeuillet and Laferrière, and two custom-made chokers containing over 2,400 diamonds. At the age of 62, Mrs Potter Palmer attended the 1911 coronation of George V in a trained court gown commissioned from Weeks of Paris.[20]

67
Jacques Doucet, 'Les Hortensias Bleus' evening dress
Silk satin and tulle, embroidered with silk, silver and sequins
Paris, 1897–1906
Galliera, Musée de la Mode de la Ville de Paris

68 *left*
**Callot Soeurs, tea gown,
worn by Emilie Grigsby**
Silk damask,
embroidered net
Paris, 1905
V&A: T.148–1967

69 *opposite*
**Poiret, mantle worn
by Emilie Grigsby**
Yellow wool lined
with black chiffon
Paris, c.1913
V&A: T.148–1967

INDIVIDUALISTS

—

While women with public positions were able to wear clothing that expressed their status, they were also constrained by the social expectations of their roles, and by the knowledge of public scrutiny. Those who were wealthy but untitled were able to express their tastes more freely, and to experiment with the latest styles. Miss Emilie Grigsby (1876–1964) was a wealthy American – with jewellery worth $800,000 in 1911 – whose equivocal relationship with a married male 'protector' scandalized contemporaries. She ran a Paris salon for artists and writers, and was a personal friend of Poiret. Her taste followed new developments in fashion, evolving from the subtle pastels and delicate textures of a 1905 Callot tea gown to the bold statement of Poiret's 1913 yellow kimono coat (pls 68 and 69).[21]

Other clients preferred a more personal engagement with the design process, specifying particular colours, fabrics or trimmings. Jacques Doucet was commissioned in 1906 by Madame André Dezarrois de La Ville le Roulx to create a gown themed around blue hydrangeas. This was in homage to the poetry collection *Les Hortensias bleus* (*The Blue Hydrangeas*), published in 1896 and 1906 by the society figure and littérateur Robert de Montesquiou (pl.67). The poet responded by dedicating a poem to Doucet, acknowledging the gown as a fitting counterpart to his verse.[22] Elisabeth de Caraman-Chimay, Comtesse Greffulhe, was a cousin of Montesquiou, and through him a friend of Marcel Proust, inspiring his character of the Duchesse de Guermantes.[23] In an 1896 photograph she is dressed in a Worth gown of black velvet appliquéd with lilies in satin and pearls, posed next to a vase of real lilies; this image was displayed by Montesquiou in a lily-embossed frame (pl.59).[24]

While large houses like Worth were able to modify designs to fit clients' requests, it was smaller and newer firms who were most able to respond to personal tastes. This can be seen in the wardrobe of Mrs Rita de Acosta Lydig (1880–1929), whose patronage of Callot Soeurs was important in establishing their business.[25] Mrs Lydig had an arresting personal appearance, extremely thin with a 'pale face dusted with lavender powder, her high collars worn tight up to the ears, her eighteenth-century tricorne hat and pointed shoes'.[26] She collected valuable antique lace, which she then commissioned Callot to work into avant-garde ensembles, combining red satin harem pants with a waistcoat of seventeenth-century Venetian lace (pl.70).

Mrs Lydig's clothes were never modern or à la mode, *belonging to no period. They were the expression of a unique personality that loved ancient brocades and velvets, was a fanatic of rare laces, and developed a style of dress to which she remained faithful despite all fashion changes. She never ordered one thing of a kind, but duplicated each item by the dozens, with only slight variations in material, lace or design. It was not unusual for twenty-five copies of one coat to be made. Mrs Lydig's adoration of clothes*

70
Callot Soeurs, evening ensemble, for Rita de Acosta Lydig
Dress with draped trousers: red silk satin; waistcoat: antique needle lace
Paris, 1913
Metropolitan Museum of Art, New York: Brooklyn Museum Costume Collection

71
**Day dress, worn by
Heather Firbank**
Linen, embroidered lawn,
embroidered net
London, c.1910
V&A: T.23–1960
**Henry of London, hat,
worn by Heather Firbank**
Black straw and artificial
flowers
London, c.1910
V&A: T.105–1960

was not for purposes of display, but because they gave her the satisfaction of a work of art.[27]

An individual sense of style could also be served by a careful selection from a range of different sources. The London socialite Miss Heather Firbank (1888–1954), daughter of Sir Thomas Firbank MP and sister of the novelist Ronald Firbank, seems to have had a preference for clothes in purples that punned on her name (pl.71). The collection of her garments from 1908 to 1921 at the V&A includes garments from Lucile, Redfern and Mascotte of London, a small firm run by Mrs Cyril Drummond.[28] The Mascotte garments supplied to Miss Firbank include a tailored suit, silk afternoon dress and cotton summer dress, all in shades of purple (pl.72). Miss Firbank's colour scheme extended to her accessories, which included purple suede walking shoes (see pl.39) and drawers in purple striped silk.[29] A more restrained form of themed dressing was practised by Mary, Viscountess Harcourt, who had a personal preference for iris motifs. The flower appears on several lace accessories in the Worth trousseau for her 1899 wedding (pl.74); she also owned a Burano needle lace stole with a deep border of irises (pl.73).

As these examples have shown, couture clients of La Belle Époque were not just passive consumers of the styles proposed by designers. In spite of Charles Frederick Worth's claims to know their needs better than they did, his clients were highly aware of the way their choice of garments would affect their public image. The fashion leaders among them tried to work with designers to create individualized designs, selecting items from collections to fit their own personal

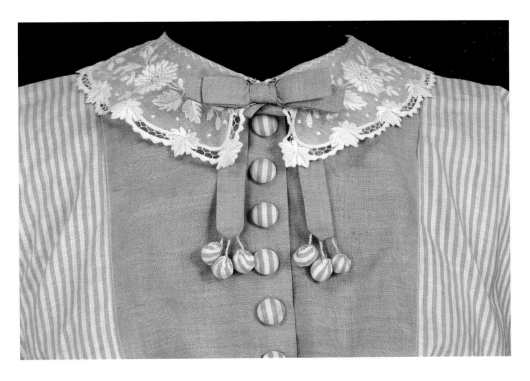

72
Mascotte, day dress, worn by Heather Firbank
Plain and striped cotton, machine-embroidered lawn
London, 1912
V&A: T.24–1960

style. Clients were also able to act as patrons, supporting and developing new businesses, and promoting them to their friends. However, the corporate and international structures of the large couture houses could make their designs rather anonymous. When Queen Alexandra preferred Indian artisans to French silk manufacturers, she was asserting her right to create her own style rather than being dictated to by professionals. This right was increasingly resisted by couturiers; from 1911, their professional body limited the changes that a client could request, in order to maintain the integrity of their designs.[30] This standardization of couture garments led, by 1927, to Chanel's little black dresses being compared to Ford motor cars: efficient, serving a multitude of purposes, and built to a common plan.[31]

73 opposite
**Stole with irises, worn
by Lady Harcourt**
Needle lace
Italy, 1900
V&A: T.29-1965

74 above & right
**Georges Robert for
Worth, lace fan leaf and
border with irises, made
for Lady Harcourt**
Silk bobbin lace
France, 1899
V&A: T.30&A-1965

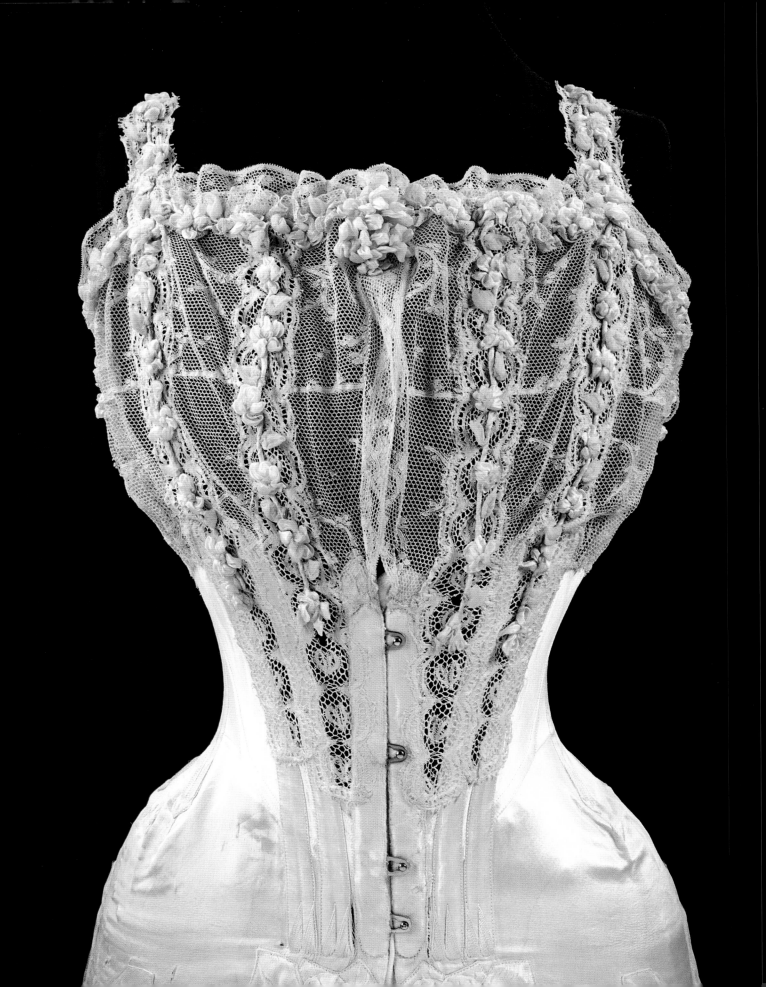

CHAPTER 5
ART NOUVEAU BODIES

—

The *fin de siècle* was a period in which the nature and extent of the support provided by foundation garments was intensely debated. Conventional practice required at least two layers of underwear between skin and outer garments at all times, prompted by hygiene – since wool suits or silk dresses were non-washable – and also by theories of health, which held that the body needed protecting from the environment. It was generally accepted that both female and male bodies needed moulding and supporting, both to produce a fashionable appearance and to alleviate the effects of physical labour.

The Rational Dress Association founded in England in 1883 had recommended that women should reduce their undergarments to a mere 3.2 kg (7 lb) in weight, including a chemise or combinations next to the skin, a supportive bodice stiffened with heavy cord, a fitted camisole, at least one long petticoat or divided skirt, and knee-length wool stockings. However, the layers of Grecian or Medieval drapery advocated by the Rational Dress Association precluded excessive exposure of the body.[1] While Paul Poiret claimed sole responsibility for the demise of corsets in fashion, stating, 'It was still the age of the corset. I waged war upon it,' it would be more accurate to say that his designs made the uncorseted body alluring.[2]

Fashionable women would need a wardrobe of underwear that corresponded to different types of garments – moderately fitted corsets and high-necked camisoles or slips with ankle-length petticoats for day; tight corsets, low-cut camisoles and trained petticoats for evening. For special occasions such as weddings, corsets decorated with lace and ribbon were produced (pl.75). Non-washable corsets needed replacing regularly, and any change in the fashionable silhouette would require a new set of underwear. The long, slender waist of the early 1890s evolved into a full-chested silhouette, which around 1900 was replaced by an S-bend shape with a straight front and curved back, followed in around 1908 by a more upright form with narrow hips. Each of these developments was presented as healthier than previous models, but each in turn revealed new problems that required correcting.[3]

The S-bend, introduced by the medically qualified Madame Gaches-Sarraute, was described by Poiret as creating 'two distinct masses: on one side there was the bust and bosom, on the other, the whole behindward aspect, so the lady looked as if she were hauling a trailer'.[4] When the tango became fashionable in 1913, shorter corsets that allowed the wearer to bend were required (pl.77). The corset of 1910 was more low-cut than ever before, requiring the addition of a bust bodice to support – or augment – the breasts (pl.76).

75
Anon., wedding corset worn by Mrs G.E. Dixon
Silk satin, whalebones, machine lace and artificial flowers
England, 1905
V&A: T90–1928

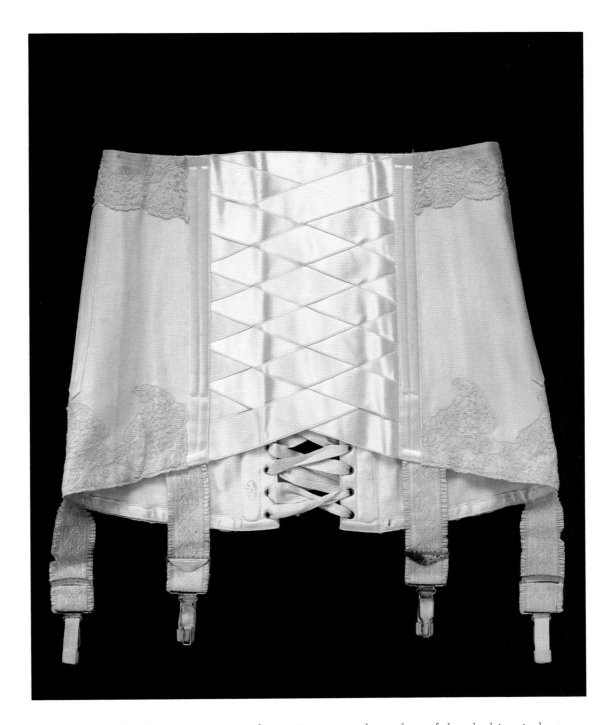

76 opposite
Anon., bust bodice
Silk satin, machine lace,
whalebone and ribbon
France, *c.*1905
V&A: T.340–1978

77 above
**Debenham & Freebody,
corset, worn by Heather
Firbank**
Cotton, machine lace,
ribbon, silk, elastic,
whalebone
France, *c.*1914
V&A: T.64–1966

Corsets and underwear in general were important branches of the clothing industry, and there were many specialist firms that provided luxurious items, like silk stockings with sequin embroidery or lace insertions (pls 78 and 79). Corsets were some of the first branded garments, widely advertised in fashion magazines and retail catalogues (pl.80). In these advertisements and in heavily retouched publicity photographs of actresses such as Camille Clifford (pl.81), the artificiality of the fashionable female silhouette was not only acknowledged but celebrated. The uncorseted body was generally seen as indecent, whether revealed by the skin-tight '*robe tanagréenne*' of Margaine-Lacroix, or skimmed over by a Poiret chemise dress (pl.83).[5] It was this that made Lucile's promotion of intimate garments in live fashion shows so shocking, particularly when the garments incorporated sheer silk fabrics and slit sides (pl.82).

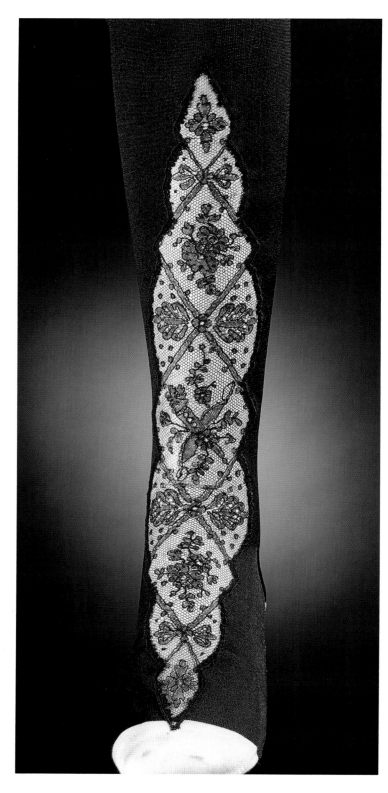

RUSTPROOF &
FULLY
GUARANTEED

BRITISH
MADE

78 *opposite left*
**Anon., stocking with lace
insertion**
Silk jersey, hand lace
Britain, *c.*1898
V&A: T.75-1951

79 *opposite right*
**Anon., stocking exhibited
at the Exposition
Universelle 1900**
Silk jersey with bead and
sequin embroidery
France, 1900
V&A: T.53-1962

80 *above*
**Anon., advertisement
for Twilfit Corsets**
Colour process engraving,
49.5 x 35.5 cm
England, *c.*1912
V&A: E.459-1916

81 *right*
**Ellis and Walery, Camille
Clifford (1885–1971), in**
The Original Gibson Girl
Hand-coloured postcard
London, 1905

82 opposite
**Lucile Ltd,
nightdress**
Silk georgette,
lace, ribbon
Britain, *c.*1913
V&A: T.1–1973

83 right
**Margaine Lacroix,
patented 'Robe Sylphide'
corsetless dress**
Pale green silk with Greek
drapery and gold
embroidery
From *Les Toilettes de la
collectivité de la Couture,
Exposition universelle
internationale de 1900*
Paris, 1900
V&A: NAL

Robe sylphide
Margaine-Lacroix

84 *above*
**Burberry & Sons,
gentleman's sports suit**
Wool flannel, cotton lining,
mother of pearl buttons
London, *c.*1904
V&A: T.159–1969

85 *right*
**Jacques Doucet, tailored
suit, worn by Mrs Ogden
Goelet**
Linen with silk embroidery
Paris, *c.*1895
V&A: T.15&A–1979

Dance, Sport and the Middle-class Body

In the early 1890s, the ideal body for upper-class women and men was neat, clearly defined and disciplined. For women this was achieved by corsets, and for men by jackets cut so closely as to constrict movement. Gentlemanly sporting activities, such as cricket, fishing, yachting and hunting, required specialist ensembles that allowed a freer range of movement, made from weather-resistant fabrics like wool flannel or tweed (pl.84). As upper-class women were encouraged by health reformers and educationalists to become more involved in sports, there was a growing range of mixed activities to dress for, including tennis, golf and bicycling.[6] This led to more specialist clothing for sportswomen – such as flexible tennis corsets or roomy golfing jackets – though these were usually offset by high collars and stiff hats, reflecting the essentially social role of middle-class sports (pl.85).

The anxieties over the limits of ladies' participation in sport was crystallized by the increasing popularity of cycling. When first introduced, this was an elite pastime, a substitute for horse-riding, with stable boys instructed to 'groom' the metal steed or to ride behind their employer.[7] It was practised in enclosed areas like country estates, city parks or indoor 'rinks', where ladies cycling in wool bloomers were protected from hostile onlookers. Nonetheless, the possible interaction between elite females and proletarian males could still cause a frisson, as in the poster for the 'Manège Central' cycling track (pl.86).

Around 1895, mass-production and technical improvements made bicycles both cheaper and safer, and cycling became more widespread and wide-ranging, practised on country lanes in Britain and the US. Ladies riding in bloomers on public roads attracted ridicule; in 1898 Lady Harberton, a strong advocate of cycling in 'rational' dress, sued a pub landlady who refused to serve her because she had not covered her bloomers with a skirt.[8]

Swimming was a sport that threatened even more bodily exposure, especially when lightweight knitted (as opposed to heavy woven) costumes were worn. Female swimmers wearing lightweight costumes were expected to cover themselves with a cloak when out of the water; this applied even to competitors in the 1908 Olympics.[9]

Gender

It was not only beauty products that were advertised with images of female bodies; one of the most noticeable themes in *fin-de-siècle* promotional images was the nude or semi-nude female body advertising traditional products such as champagne, and goods that epitomized modernity such as cigarettes or bicycles (see pl.1).[10] Very often, these bodies were presented in ways that made them promoters of an active, even threatening sexuality, rather than passive recipients of male fantasy. Heroines from ancient history and legend – Astarte, Judith, Medea, Salome and Cleopatra – were depicted by artists such as Klimt, Khnopff, Moreau and Beardsley in scenes that emphasized their power over men.[11]

The corollary of the dominant woman was the submissive or emasculated man; campaigns for women's rights in education, employment and the vote were mocked with

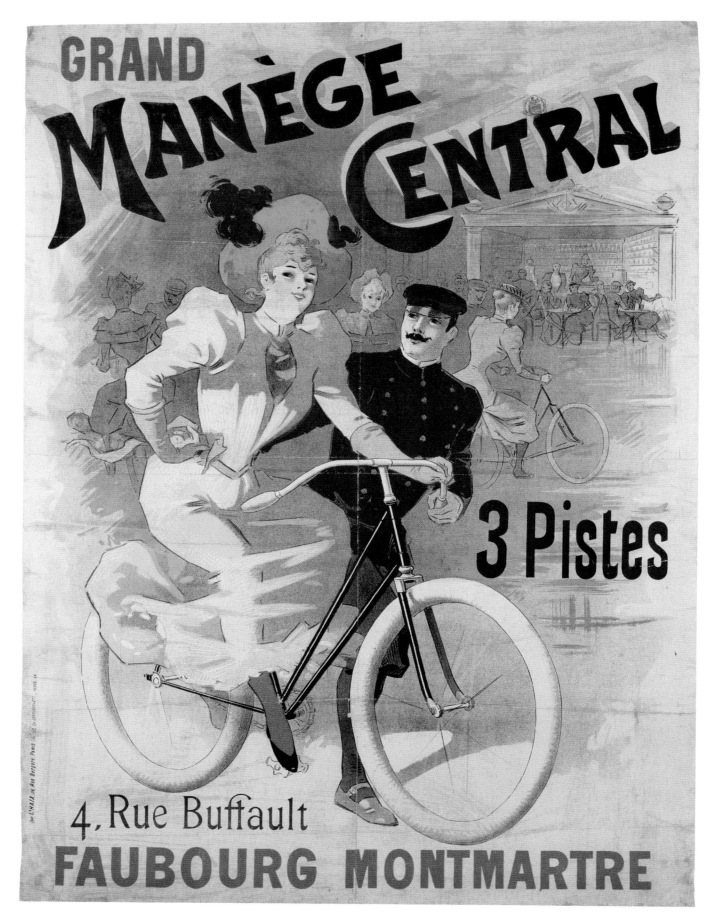

86 *opposite*
Lucien Baylac, 'Grand Manège Central'
Colour lithograph poster,
123.5 x 88 cm
Paris, 1894
V&A: E.148–1921

87 *above*
Aubrey Beardsley,
'The Peacock Skirt'
Half-tone print, 34 x 27 cm
From *Salome* [1894]
London, 1907
V&A: E.426–1972

cartoons of hen-pecked husbands. This fear of female domination was fostered by the increasing number of women teachers and clerical workers who adopted 'masculine' tailored suits, stiff collars and ties for their professional dress. Thus even couture versions of the tailored suit carried suggestions of female empowerment and gender subversion (pl.85).

While the variety of human sexuality was being investigated theoretically by Richard von Krafft-Ebing (*Psychopathia Sexualis*, 1886) and Sigmund Freud (*Studies on Hysteria*, 1895), in practice sexual irregularity was both stigmatized and criminalized. The conviction and imprisonment of Oscar Wilde for homosexuality in 1895 tainted the individuals and causes with which he was associated. Aubrey Beardsley had illustrated Wilde's banned play *Salome* in 1894; in the aftermath of the trial Beardsley was dismissed from his post as art editor of the *Yellow Book* magazine, which published avant-garde literature and illustrations (pl.87).[12]

Wilde's advocacy of greater variety in clothing for men, and greater freedom in dress for women, also suffered by association. Elite male dress codes in the 1890s centred on the wearing of correct garments for specific occasions, from the early morning ride in the park to the evening ball. Greater liberty was permissible in clothing for wear at home, such as the Indian silk smoking suit worn by Jack Eden (elder brother of the Prime Minister Anthony Eden) (pl.88) or the hand-embroidered waistcoat worn by Henry Paget, Marquess of Anglesey (pl.89). Accessories such as neckties were also a focus for fashionable variation, and new styles were produced every season by manufacturers such as Welch Margetson (pl.90). However, for public appearances the overall ethos was one of harmonious restraint. As Proust wrote of the Baron de Charlus, based on the littérateur Comte Robert de Montesquiou:

> One felt that if colour was almost entirely absent from these garments it was not because he who had banished it from them was indifferent to it ... A dark green thread harmonized, in the stuff of his trousers, with the clock on his socks, with a refinement that betrayed the vivacity of a taste that was everywhere else conquered, to which this single concession had been made.[13] (pl.91)

In London, the artificial nature of elite male appearance was highlighted by the popularity of music-hall sketches making fun of working-class 'mashers'. There were also female performers who specialized in impersonating male characters, from upper-class dandies to adolescent naval cadets. The best-known of these, Vesta Tilley, was able to preserve an appropriately feminine offstage persona and married a Conservative Member of Parliament, yet her stage costume included clothing from the estate of the Marquess of Anglesey, and her name was used to sell male accessories such as hats and waistcoats (pl.92).[14]

88
Anon., smoking suit, worn by Jack Eden
Indian printed silk lined in wool
Britain, c.1906
V&A: T.720–1974

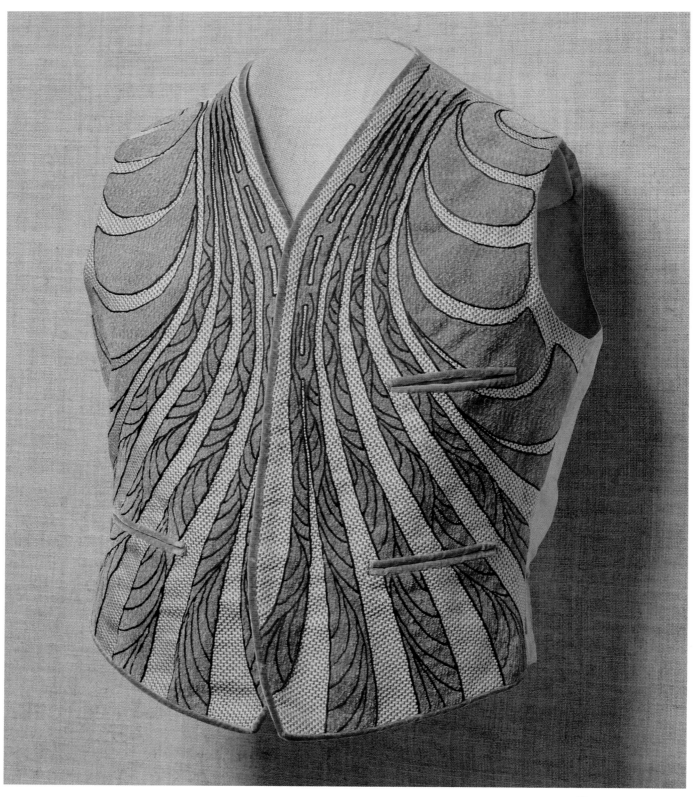

89

**H. Creed & Co.,
embroidered waistcoat, for
the Marquess of Anglesey**
Cotton canvas embroidered
in cotton and chenille
threads, silk lined
Paris, 1900–04
V&A: T.177–1967

*A large range in 1-inch and 2-inch Check Twills
in light and dark colourings.*

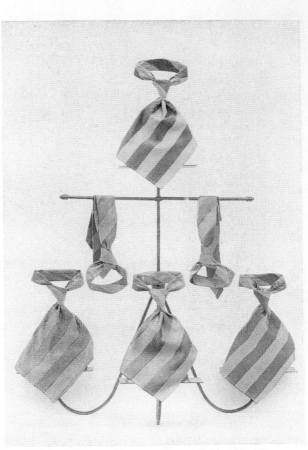

*A large range in 1-inch and 2-inch Stripe Twills
in light and dark colourings.*

90
**Welch Margetson & Co.
Ltd, sample book for
gentlemen's accessories**
London, 1908
V&A: T.80–1981

91 *opposite*
Giovanni Boldini, *Comte Robert de Montesquiou*
Oil painting, 116 x 82.5 cm
France, 1897
Musée d'Orsay, Paris

92 *right*
Sheet music cover, 'Burlington Bertie by Harry B. Norris, as sung by Vesta Tilley'
London, c.1900
V&A: S.81-2008,
Gabrielle Enthoven Collection

Sarah Bernhardt

—

One public figure who epitomized threatening female sexuality was the actress Sarah Bernhardt. From the start of her career she was associated with roles portraying sexually compromised women such as Marguerite in Alexandre Dumas's *La Dame aux caméllias*. As her reputation grew, she commissioned star vehicles in which she played tragic heroines from history, legend or scripture – Medea, the Empress Theodora, Cleopatra (pl.94). Oscar Wilde's *Salome* (1891) was written in French with Bernhardt in mind as the heroine whose erotic obsession with John the Baptist leads to tragedy. Bernhardt was not satisfied with female roles alone; she also played the male leads in *Hamlet* and *Romeo and Juliet*, and premiered Edmond Rostand's play *L'Aiglon* as the eponymous 'Eaglet', Napoleon's doomed son, for which she wore a breeches suit designed by the young Paul Poiret.[15]

In her private life Bernhardt also challenged acceptable gender roles – not so much by the sexual liaisons expected of actresses, but by practising as a fine artist, creating bronze sculptures that were exhibited in the Salon of 1876 and the Exposition Universelle 1900.[16] Bernhardt wore a trouser suit for work in her studio – an impractical white silk one, specially commissioned from Worth – and had publicity photographs taken in this attire. Another publicity photograph of Bernhardt showed her lying seemingly dead in a coffin, sparking a rumour that she slept in a casket.[17] Even when dressed and posed conventionally, Bernhardt's extreme slenderness and pallor gave her a neurotic appearance heightened by accessories such as the serpent bracelet she commissioned from Mucha in 1899 (pl.93), referencing her portrayal of the femmes fatales Cleopatra and Medea.[18]

Loïe Fuller

—

Even more than the drama, dance spectacles presented audiences with new ways of visualizing both female and male bodies. Into the 1890s, female costumes for classical ballet included tight-fitting, even corseted bodices, with the main concession to movement being skirts shortened to just below the knee.[19] From the 1890s, however, new styles of artistic dance relied on aesthetic rather than sexualized visions of the body.

One of the most prominent female dancers was Loïe Fuller (1860–1928), an American performer who adapted the full skirt worn in the popular 'serpentine dance' so that it covered her whole body from the neck downwards and stretched for several metres beyond her feet. Although Fuller was dressed only in a body stocking under this skirt, the attraction of her performances lay not in glimpses of her rather dumpy body but in the extraordinary effects she created by setting in motion up to 500 square metres of lightweight silk, manipulating it by long canes held in her hands.[20] Fuller devised special lighting effects and mirrored stage sets to enhance the impression of flames, flowers and clouds created by the moving fabric, and her stage shows were praised by leading artists and critics.

Fuller's dances were represented not only on promotional posters by Jules Chéret (pl.95), but also in art prints by Toulouse Lautrec, and in manufactured objects, including electric lamps by Larche, and jewellery. A series of Sèvres statuettes which won a prize in the Exposition Universelle 1900 depicted Fuller's 'Scarf Dance' in forms based on Tanagra ceramics made in fourth-century BC Greece (pl.96).[21] At the Exposition Fuller performed in her own theatre, decorated with a sculpture of her figure in motion, and with plaster reliefs representing waves of drapery. Jean Cocteau commented: 'From this dusty and confused fair, I retain only one vibrant and flamboyant image: Madame Loïe Fuller . . . Let us salute this dancer . . . this phantom of an era'.[22]

It could be argued that Fuller's presentation of a female body – neither clothed nor undressed but moving in harmony with its drapery – represented the realization of the ideals of dress reformers. Fuller's influence on conventional fashion can be seen in the adoption of dresses with full pleated skirts (worn over supportive undergarments) for young middle-class girls attending dance parties. She may also have inspired the radical rethinking of adult female garments presented by Mariano Fortuny (1871–1949) (pl.99). Fortuny's finely-pleated 'Delphos' gowns also drew on interpretations of Greek art in modern dance, notably by Isadora Duncan. Duncan, who had worked with Fuller, performed onstage in a scandalously short Greek tunic and bare legs, and wore Fortuny garments offstage.[23]

RUSSIAN BALLET AND FASHION

A much more direct effect on fashion can be seen from the dance performances staged by Serge Diaghilev's Ballets Russes in Paris and London from 1909. After their appearance, *Le Courrier musical*, an established music journal, and its new rival *Comoedia illustré*, started to run regular features on fashion at the theatre, illustrated with portraits of couture-clad stars.[24] Diaghilev productions were notable for their innovative design, with music, choreography, scenery, costumes and story creating an integrated whole. The themes chosen were often exotic and erotic: the 1909 Paris season presented dancers dressed as central Asian warriors (*Prince Igor*) and as Egyptian courtiers (*Cleopatra*), and the 1910 season staged a Russian fairytale (*Firebird*) and an orgy in a harem (*Schéhérazade*).[25] The latter was notable for costumes with sheer harem pants and brief tops which appeared to bare the dancers' midriffs and arms (actually covered with tinted silk body stockings) (pl.98).

Orientalist costumes were also popular for fancy dress balls, where participants could indulge their sartorial fantasies; although held in private, they were often photographed for the illustrated press.[26] The prevalence of orientalist dramas and dances may have influenced attitudes to visible make-up; this had not previously been acceptable offstage, but by 1911 even Paquin was producing fashion sketches where the models were wearing Oriental slippers – and dark eye-liner (see pl.16). This was the last stage of the beauty aids that had been produced and advertised since the 1890s, often endorsed by leading actresses (see Chapter 4).[27] Scientific testimonials were used to promote weight-correction

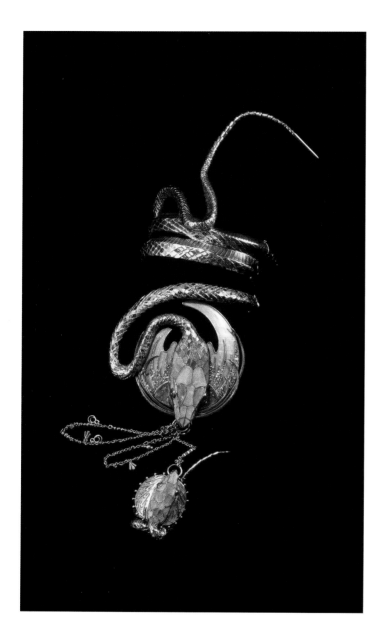

93 *above*
Alphonse Mucha and Georges Fouquet, serpent bracelet and hand decoration, made for Sarah Bernhardt
Gold, enamel, opals, rubies and diamonds
Paris, 1899
Sakai City Collection

94 *right*
Alphonse Mucha, 'Médée'
Colour lithograph poster,
205.7 x 74 cm
Paris, 1898
V&A: E.1000–1963

95 *above*
**Jules Chéret,
'Folies-Bergère–
La Loïe Fuller'**
Colour lithograph poster,
124 x 87 cm
France, 1893
V&A: E.112–1921

96 *right*
**Agathon Léonard for
Sèvres, Jeu de l'écharpe,
ceramic figurine**
Biscuit porcelain
France, 1900
V&A: C.89A–1971

pills (both reducing and increasing) and gadgets such as water-powered massage devices or electric hairdryers and curling tongs (pl.97).

Thus the fashionable body in 1890–1914 was not a natural entity, but one that was produced through the application of corsetry, clothing and cosmetics. New pastimes, such as bicycling and tango dancing, required specific types of movement – which in turn required new types of clothing. For women claiming the right to participate more fully in the professions and in politics, there were tailored garments that shocked onlookers with their masculinity. At the same time, the ultra-feminine lingerie promoted by designers such as Lucile was controversial in its frank appeal to the senses. Each of these extremes highlighted the arbitrariness of contemporary gendered dress codes, preparing the way for more radical changes in practices after 1914.

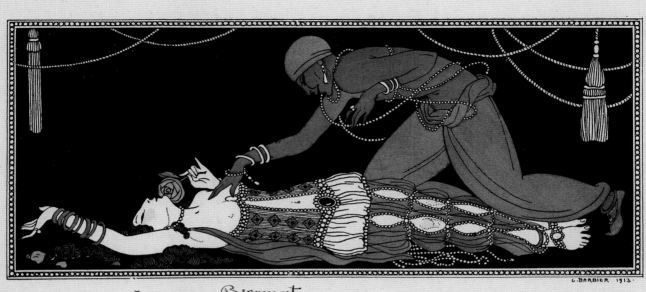

à monsieur Beaumont
très sympathiquement
George Barbier

97 *opposite*
**'Electricity in the
Bedroom', Electric Supply
Publicity Co. Leaflet 1900**
National Archives, Kew

98 *above*
**Georges Barbier, Vaslav
Nijinsky and Ida Rubinstein
in Schéhérazade**
Colour print, 24.5 x 32 cm
Paris, 1913
V&A: S.15–2001

99 *right*
**Mariano Fortuny,
'Delphos' dress (detail),
worn by Eleonora Duse**
Pleated and block printed
silk, glass beads
Italy, *c.*1912
V&A: T.731–1972

CHAPTER 6
ARTISTS & ART NOUVEAU FASHION

—

As discussed in the Introduction, between 1890 and 1914 dress was granted the status of a decorative art, shown at exhibitions, published in magazines[1], and included in many of the theoretical debates about the purpose of art in everyday life. Many fine artists collaborated with individual designers, either to provide illustrations of finished garments, or to create the fabrics and forms of the garments themselves. For example, the 1901 Exhibition of the Société Nationale des Beaux-Arts in Paris included a silk dress made from fabric painted by the artist Victor Prouvé. Conversely, many fashion designers saw themselves as artists: Charles Worth was photographed in a loose robe and beret, and his garments were signed like works of art.[2]

From 1884, French law gave fashion designers the right to claim protection for their work under the 'droit d'auteur' held by creative artists.[3] However, this right was hard to enforce, especially in the US, where the copying of designs for mass-production was widespread. When Poiret tried to take action against copyists, the American court ruled that fashion was not art, and only the designer's label could be copyrighted.[4] Less problematically, leading couturiers acted as patrons of fine art, with Jacques Doucet known as a collector specializing in the seventeenth and eighteenth centuries, and Paul Poiret as an organizer of contemporary art exhibitions. As one example, Pablo Picasso's iconoclastic 1907 *Demoiselles d'Avignon* was first shown to the public at an event staged in Poiret's couture salon in 1916, and was eventually sold to Doucet in 1924.[5]

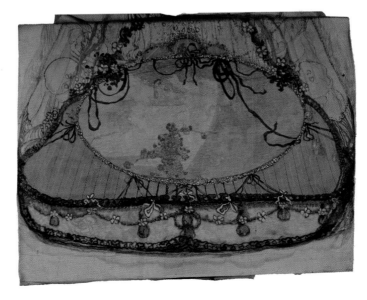

opposite
Gustav Klimt, *Emilie*
Flöge **(detail of pl.108)**

100 right
**Charles Conder, train
for evening dress (detail)**
Watercolour on silk,
188 x 109 cm
London, 1903
V&A: E.2380–1930

ARTISTS DESIGNING FASHION

—

The delicate surfaces of elite Art Nouveau fashion provided opportunities for fine artists. The Anglo-Australian artist Charles Conder (1868–1909), who designed some interiors for Siegfried Bing's *Maison de l'Art Nouveau*, also executed hand-painted silk panels for fans and dresses. These show a delicate, rococo revival style quite different from his impressionistic landscapes (pl.100).[6] Very fragile, and with their exquisite detail only apparent at a close distance, these would have been extravagant commissions.[7]

The Spanish painter Mariano Fortuny y Madrazo moved from the production of canvases and engravings to designing for the theatre, and from 1906 to the production of innovative garments influenced by his studies of classical Greek and Medieval costumes and his personal collection of Near-Eastern garments. His theatrical experience is reflected in the processes he used to decorate outer garments, with gold paint imitating sumptuous Renaissance velvets (see pl.99). More fundamentally, Fortuny's creation of garments that stood outside the conventional fashion cycle was a strategy common to providers of 'artistic' dress in the nineteenth century. However, this 'artistic' style of dress was criticized as an affectation, as Adolf Loos pointed out in an 1898 article on men's fashion:

101
**Liberty & Co.,
evening coat**
Silk, embroidered trim,
'Aurora' silk lining
London, 1905
V&A: T.36–2007

102 *top*
**Forma for Liberty & Co.,
dress**
Silk crepe and
embroidered velvet
London, 1905
V&A: T.638–1964

103 *bottom*
**Henry van de Velde,
two women in 'reform'
dresses**
From *Deutsche Kunst und
Dekoration*, April–
September 1902
V&A: NAL

Germans from the best society side with the English. They are satisfied if they are dressed well. They abjure claims to beauty. The great poet, the great painter, the great architect dress like the English. The would-be poet, the would-be master painter, the budding architect, on the other hand, make temples of their bodies in which beauty in the form of velvet collars, aesthetic trouser fabric, and Secessionist neckties is to be worshipped.[8]

Liberty & Co. had opened a dressmaking department in 1884, with the respected designer William Godwin (1833–86) as advisor, aiming to produce 'artistic' clothing based on distant times or cultures.[9] By 1900 they were producing catalogues for both 'Costumes Never out of Fashion' and 'Novelties for the New Season'.[10] One dress designed around 1910 by Forma for Liberty interpreted the current silhouette of long, slender lines and a raised waist through a medieval tabard (pl.102). 'Artistic' garments were often distinguished by the use of boldly patterned or exotic fabrics, offset by a simplified cut (pl.101). Some of Liberty's exclusive fabrics were very high-priced; warp-painted 'Aurora' silk retailed at 8s 6d per yard at a time when working men might earn only 20s per week.

As with many aspects of Art Nouveau, the relationship between artists and fashion grew out of the practices of the British Arts and Crafts movement. The leading example was that of William Morris, whose homes at Red House and then at Kelmscott presented a harmony of architecture, decoration and the clothing of the (female) inhabitants.[11] The Belgian artist Henry van de Velde was inspired by Morris in 1894 to build a family home in which:

every element of the design, from door handles to wall paper, from candelabra to chairs, assumed the same flowing linear shape and was adorned with the same patterned embellishment. Van de Velde's purpose was to fashion an ensemble in which all the components of both inner and outer design would form interdependent elements of a single spatial whole.[12]

As part of this total artwork, Van de Velde designed dresses for his wife (pl.103). A surviving example in the Design Museum, Ghent, is made from dark blue cotton velvet, flowing without a waist seam from a contrasting yoke decorated with Art Nouveau patterns.[13] This construction complied with current thinking about the need for 'reformed' dress to avoid pressure on the chest and waist (even though the light-coloured example in pl.103 seems to be worn over a figure-defining corset). Fortuitously, it also gave the designer a large uninterrupted area on which to place his decoration. Van de Velde's ideas gained currency through his participation in high-profile projects such as Bing's pavilion at the Exposition Universelle 1900. He also wrote about art and design, lamenting in 1902 that 'the outer cover of all constructed things (by which I mean everything from a house to an item of clothing) has long since lost all integrity and organic expression; it lives its own life entirely unrelated to its environment'.[14]

Glasgow

Even more influential on concepts of dress as art were the designers associated with the Glasgow School of Art: architects, fine artists, decorative artists and educators whose work shared an identifiable style. This school had an integrated approach to the arts, with all students following the same introductory course before specializing in areas which – from 1895 – included the applied arts of metalwork, bookbinding, needlework and decorative painting. These areas were especially attractive to female students and female tutors, including Jessie Rowat Newbery, wife of the School's director. While the architect Hermann Muthesius was researching the latest developments in British architecture in 1902–3, his wife Anna was so taken with the clothes made and worn by Glasgow designers that she published a book on unique and artistic clothing, *Das Eigenkleid der Frau*, with a cover and illustrations based on designs by Margaret Macdonald Mackintosh, her sister Frances Macdonald MacNair, and Jessie Newbery.[15]

From 1899 the Glasgow School of Art ran evening classes in embroidery for women school teachers (who were expected to teach needlework). These classes spread their innovative designs and techniques and contributed to the recruitment of more female students, who formed 47 per cent of the student body by 1902. Jessie Newbery advocated the use of simple materials and a limited repertoire of stitches so that the design of the work remained paramount

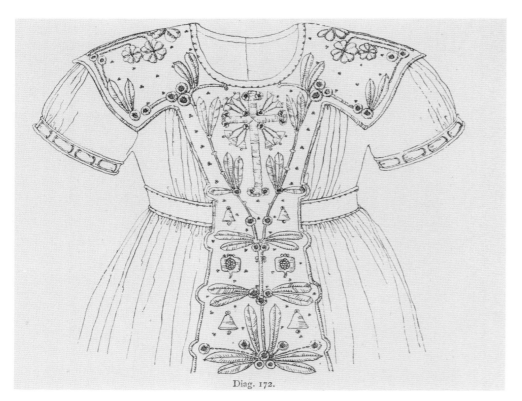

Diag. 172.

104 *left*
Ann Macbeth, embroidery design for christening gown
From Margaret Swanson and Ann Macbeth, *Educational Needlecraft* London, 1913

105 *top*
Jessie Newbery, collar
Silk, silk appliqué and embroidery, beads
Glasgow, c.1900
V&A: Circ.189-1953

106 *bottom*
Jessie Newbery, maternity dress
Silk, silk appliqué and embroidery, beads
Glasgow, 1902
Gallery of Costume, Manchester City Galleries

(pl.105). Her designs for dress accessories such as collars and waistbands were placed on simply constructed garments influenced by the ideas of dress reformers (pl.106).

These ideas were continued by Newbery's successor Ann Macbeth, whose 1911 textbook *Educational Needlecraft* gave diagrams and lesson plans for teaching Glasgow-style embroidery to children aged four and upwards (pl.104).[16] The work of this department showed a remarkable commitment to the integration of dress and the decorative arts, and to making art available to all, not just the leisured elite – ideals that were developed in the work of the Bauhaus in the 1920s and 1930s.

In addition to designers trained specifically in embroidery, many Glasgow alumni prominent in other fields also produced designs for jewellery, dress accessories and textiles.[17] This was partly a result of the school's commitment to an integrated aesthetic approach in all media. As a reviewer recognized in 1900, the harmony of rooms designed by Charles Rennie Mackintosh (1868–1928) and Margaret Macdonald Mackintosh (1865–1933) would have been destroyed by inhabitants in fashionable garments:

You have seen Mrs Mackintosh herself, standing in the room like a Gothic pillar. Her hat was the capital, the perpendicular folds of her long mantle providing the fluting. Just imagine Mrs Mackintosh standing in blouse with wide, bulky sleeves, in a jacket that exaggerated the hips; imagine the pictures on the walls replaced by others . . . it will feel like a slap in the face. The stylistic unity of the room has become manifest to you![18]

There were also pragmatic reasons for artists' involvement in designs for textiles and fashion accessories, as these could easily be sold to manufacturers and retailers at times when commissions for larger decorative projects were scarce. The illustrator Jessie M. King sold designs for silver and enamel jewellery to Liberty. Mackintosh had been producing jewellery designs since 1900; during the First World War he lived mainly from his textile designs (pl.107).

107
**Charles Rennie
Mackintosh, design
for textile border**
Drawing with watercolour,
13.5 x 13.5 cm
Glasgow, 1918
V&A: E.854–1968

THE WIENER WERKSTÄTTE

Glasgow-trained designers often shared exhibition spaces and patrons with members of the Munich, Berlin and Vienna 'Secession' groups of artists and designers, founded between 1892 and 1898 in protest against the conservatism of local art establishments. Each of these groups held exhibitions in their own galleries, and their work was also publicized in avant-garde magazines such as *Pan* (Berlin) and *Ver Sacrum* (Vienna), and by participation in international expositions and design competitions.

The teaching by Vienna Secession members such as Koloman Moser and Josef Hoffmann, both professors at the Vienna Kunstgewerbeschule (School of Applied Arts), was also instrumental in spreading new ideas.[19] It was a realization of the commercial potential of these new styles that led to the foundation of the Wiener Werkstätte by Fritz Waerndorfer, an industrialist who had commissioned interior designs from Charles Rennie and Margaret Macdonald Mackintosh. Influenced by the ideals of the British Arts and Crafts movement, the Wiener Werkstätte was set up as a co-operative, with the designers sharing in the profits. These included leading Secessionists such as the fine artists Gustav Klimt and Egon Schiele, the architect Josef Hoffmann and the designer Koloman Moser, alongside young designers recruited from art colleges.[20]

Early commissions for the Wiener Werkstätte included a showroom for the Viennese couturiers Emilie, Pauline and Helene Flöge (1904), which was decorated with rectilinear furnishings and minimalist shades of grey and silver which formed a background to the avant-garde garments.[21] These were simply constructed from fabrics whose patterns of squares and spirals owed a debt to the backgrounds of the paintings of Gustav Klimt (pl.108). This was not surprising, as Helene Flöge had married Klimt's brother, and Emilie was a close friend and muse. A 1906 profile of Klimt included ten photographs of Flöge wearing dresses designed by the artist.[22]

The importance of fashion in the design thinking of the Wiener Werkstätte was confirmed when they opened a fashion department in 1910.[23] This was apparently prompted by the clash between the decoration designed by the Wiener Werkstätte in 1905–11 for the Stoclet family's Brussels townhouse, and the fashionable clothing worn by Madame Stoclet.[24] The fashion workshop, led by the artist Eduard Wimmer-Wisgrill, produced distinctive, brightly patterned printed dress textiles and accessories that were made up into ensembles that presented a simplified interpretation of current fashions (pl.109). Berta Zuckerkandel, an art critic and patron, commented in 1916:

> *It was logical that the spirit of the Klimt group should lead to the creation of the Wiener Werkstätte dress. The leading artists of Vienna have raised the frippery of fashion to a noble craft. They have even created outstanding fabrics, unique in colour and ornamentation, for their original*

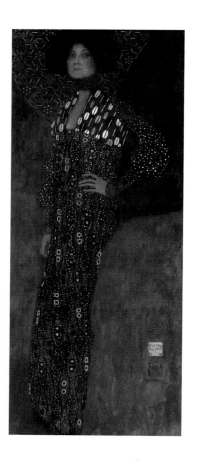

108
Gustav Klimt, *Emilie Flöge*
Oil on canvas, 172 x 80 cm
Vienna, 1902
Wien Museum

109 *above left*
Eduard Wimmer-Wisgrill, blouse
Printed silk (designed by Ugo Zovetti), lace, pearl buttons
Wiener Werkstätte, Vienna, c.1915
V&A: T.47–2004

110 *above right*
Atelier Martine for Paul Poiret, block-printed silk fabrics
Paris, 1919
V&A: T.539 to 541–1919

designs. They have utterly changed the concept of accessories through the batik sashes, knitted belts and novel passementerie [braid trimming]. They have taught us to realise that design determines the character of the dress. These dresses, coats, sashes and hats work because they are decorative distillations of an idea of our time. Through careful, conscious design, fashion has become style.[25]

This aim was furthered by press coverage of stands at international expositions, and by the sale of postcards of designs to clients who might not be able to buy the originals (pl.112). Hundreds of postcard designs were produced, and at international exhibitions in Rome in 1911 and Cologne in 1914 they were used to cover an entire wall of the Wiener Werkstätte display area (pl.111).

PARIS COUTURE AND ARTISTS

The Wiener Werkstätte were highly influential in international design, inspiring the British Omega Workshops set up in 1913 by the art critic Roger Fry, with designs by the artists Duncan Grant and Vanessa Bell. However, with little technical expertise their output remained rather amateurish in quality and limited in extent, and Omega closed in 1919.[26] More successful was Poiret's

111
**Wiener Werkstätte
installation at the
Deutscher Werkbund
exhibition, Cologne, 1914**
Museum für angewandte
Kunst, Vienna

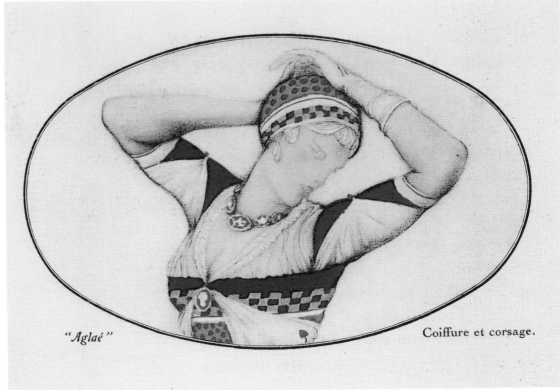

"Aglaé"   Coiffure et corsage.

112 *above*
**Mela Koehler, fashion
design postcard**
Wiener Werkstätte,
Vienna, 1911
Museum für angewandte
Kunst, Vienna

113 *right*
**Leon Bakst, 'Aglaé' dress
made up by Paquin**
Fashion plate (pochoir
print), *Gazette du bon ton*,
vol.1, no.6 (1912)

114
**Paul Iribe, fashion plate
(pochoir print)**
From *Les Robes de Paul
Poiret racontées par Paul
Iribe*
Paris, 1908

Atelier Martine for textile design, founded in 1911 following a visit to Vienna (pl.110). Poiret deliberately eschewed the art-school roots of the Viennese workshop, recruiting only untrained girls to his atelier; nevertheless, the designs produced by the two workshops were similar enough to be confused by publications such as *Vogue*.[27]

Poiret's insistence on untrained designers represented a new departure, as he had previously engaged painters and graphic artists to produce textiles and promotional images (pl.114). The best known of these was Raoul Dufy, a Fauvist artist who from 1911 designed textiles first for Poiret's exclusive use, and later for sale by the silk manufacturer Bianchini-Férier of Lyons (see pl.20).[28]

Madame Paquin went further than this when in 1913 she made up a range of garments designed by the artist Leon Bakst, best known as the originator of orientalist costumes for Diaghilev's Ballets Russes. The results were presented in *Vogue* and the *Gazette du bon ton* as fashionable clothing, but were so striking that it is unlikely any copies were sold (pl.113). Paquin then reinforced her links to the ballet company by providing costumes based on sports clothes for *Jeux*, a piece choreographed by Vaslav Nijinsky.[29] *The New York Times* commented: 'No French dressmaker would admit for a fleeting second that she could bring herself down to anything so inartistic as advertisement. She [Paquin] maintains the attitude of an artist, but we know that she is the most commercial artist alive.'[30]

Still more radical was the 'simultaneous' dress made by the artist Sonia Delaunay in the same year. This interpreted the abstract geometry of her paintings in panels of different coloured fabrics arranged so that they formed kaleidoscopic patterns when the wearer moved. This experiment was later followed by a range of clothing with abstract patterns worked in embroidery or knitting, sold through her own boutiques, and in collaboration with couturiers such as Jacques Doucet.[31]

Thus, in the period from 1890 to 1914 fashion designers and fine artists were working on several different initiatives that established dress as art. Some fashionable garments had elements created by fine artists, or were presented to the public through images that had the status of art. Artists were highly aware of clothing as an aspect of interior decoration, and produced designs that harmonized with their surroundings. Some artists went even further in producing designs that made the clothed body into a moving canvas of abstract patterns. This recognition of dress as art would be one of the key themes of the Art Nouveau revival of the 1960s and 1970s.

CHAPTER 7

ART NOUVEAU REVIVAL

—

After 1914 the different strains within Art Nouveau fashion – exoticism, eroticism, dress as art, and innovative approaches to materials and techniques – were increasingly sidelined by the exigencies of war. While the grand couture houses remained open, their business was damaged by wartime conditions that made it difficult for international clients to visit Paris. There were difficulties in accessing high-quality materials (notably dyestuffs, for which Germany was the world leader), and in holding on to skilled workshop staff.[1] In addition to all these practical obstacles, there was a change in mentality, with elite clients whose lives had previously been framed in terms of conspicuous consumption retrenching their expenditure and volunteering for nursing and other support work – when they were not mourning those lost in battle.[2]

French couturiers played on this new mentality to push new designs with shorter, fuller skirts dubbed 'war crinolines', and succeeded in increasing the numbers of dresses exported during 1915 and 1916 – and increasing prices as well. At the same time, wages for (mainly female) workers in couture had been reduced by as much as 50 per cent in order to safeguard jobs, while jobs in war industries such as munitions were well-paid. This disjunction led to a strike of 31,000 garment workers in May 1917 and to a more adversarial relationship between employers and staff thereafter.[3]

Wartime uncertainties also led to long-lasting shifts within the fashion industry, with the rise of new designers such as Chanel specializing in casual or 'sports' clothing – and the growing independence of American and British designers from French fashion leaders.[4] By 1927, when *Vogue* saluted Chanel's go-anywhere black dress as fashion's answer to the Model T Ford, the overall design ethos was that of Modernism, with simplified shapes and an emphasis on functionality and ease of movement.[5] Art Nouveau was seen as not only outmoded but aesthetically and morally harmful: a 1933 architectural critic decried Charles Rennie Mackintosh's 'partial adherence to that baneful "Art Nouveau" movement . . . this side of his work was the result of his wife's influence'.[6] This distaste for Art Nouveau may have been linked to its identification by Salvador Dalí as a precursor to Surrealism in a 1933 article on the 'terrifying' and 'edible' beauty of the architecture of Gaudí.[7]

In 1956, however, the art historian Stephan Tschudi Madsen's book *Sources of Art Nouveau* led the intellectual rehabilitation of Art Nouveau, distinguishing between national variants of the style.[8] The aesthetic revival of Art Nouveau began in 1959, with the landmark exhibition Art Nouveau: Art and Design at the Turn of the Century at the Museum of Modern Art, New York. This was followed in 1960 by a Council of Europe sponsored exhibition on the Sources du

115
Arthur Sanderson & Sons Ltd, Aubrey Beardsley collage
Roller-printed wallpaper, 51-cm wide, 92-cm repeat
England, 1967
V&A E.405–1998

XXe Siècle in Paris, the catalogue of which was notably ambivalent towards Art Nouveau, identifying it with 'parasitic' applied decoration, stylistic 'impurity', and brashly insistent bad taste.[9] It was this lack of conventional good taste and refusal to conform to the tenets of Modernism that led Susan Sontag to identify Art Nouveau as 'the most typical and fully developed Camp style' in her 1964 essay 'Notes on Camp'. In this reading, the sexually perverse elements of the style became part of its attraction. *Time* magazine was already discussing a revival of Art Nouveau in 1964, although in the US this was largely confined to an interest in artefacts such as Tiffany glassware.[10] In France, interest in the lavish materials, fine craftsmanship and symbolic references present in Art Nouveau jewellery and decorative art was fostered by illustrated books by the art expert and dealer Maurice Rheims published in 1964 and 1965.

Popular interest in Art Nouveau graphics was confirmed by exhibitions at the V&A of the work of Alphonse Mucha (1963) and Aubrey Beardsley (1966). The Beardsley retrospective was recognized at the time as especially attractive to the young, with George Melly, the jazz musician and art critic, remembering it as:

116 *opposite*
Paul Christadoulou, poster for Elliott 'Alice' boots
Lithograph, 76 x 101.5 cm
London, c.1966
V&A: E.12–1967

117 *right*
Wes Wilson, 'Byrds Byrds Byrds' poster advertising concerts in San Francisco, 31 March to 2 April 1967
Colour lithograph,
57 x 35 cm
San Francisco, 1967
V&A: E.396–1968

packed with people . . . Many were clearly art students, some were Beats,
others could have been pop musicians, most of them were very young, but
almost all of them gave the impression of belonging to a secret society which
had not yet declared its aims and intentions. I believe now . . . that I had
stumbled for the first time into the presence of the emerging Underground.[11]

Within months Beardsley designs had been adapted for interior décor,
including a Sanderson wallpaper composed of a montage of his 'greatest hits'
(pl.115). Beardsley-influenced figures were used to advertise laced ankle boots
by the British retailer Elliott, with satyrs and semi-nude dancers underscoring
the Victorian styling of the product (pl.116). The insistent sexuality of these
figures was still seen as shocking: even during the V&A exhibition, a shop
selling Beardsley prints was raided by the Vice Squad.[12] A London barbershop
called Samson and Delilah titillated male customers with the double attraction
of a mural combining Beardsley and the Kama Sutra, and female staff dressed
in mini-dresses with cut-away midriffs.[13]

In the US, Art Nouveau was a major influence on the publicity materials
of the West Coast music scene from at least 1965, though the references were
not to Beardsley's monochromes but rather to the stylized figures and fluid
compositions of Mucha. Particularly when re-coloured in intense pinks, purples
and oranges, these images glowed and vibrated in a way that matched the light
shows at psychedelic music events (pl.117).[14] An article in *Time* coined the term
'Nouveau Frisco' to describe this style: 'From coast to coast, be-ins, folk-rock
festivals, art galleries and department-store sales are now advertised in posters
and layouts done in a style that is beginning to be called Nouveau Frisco.'[15]

The Art Nouveau revival also received support from non-European design
sources. Turn-of-the century design had been inflected by cultures on the
fringes of or beyond Europe, with Celtic knotwork, Scandinavian dragon
interlace, Indian plant motifs and Japanese asymmetry all prominent. The
construction methods of 'peasant' clothing had also provided an important
alternative to conventionally fitted garments. In the 1960s, young designers
returned to these models either through travel on the 'hippie trail' to Africa,
India and the Far East or through historic documents. Zandra Rhodes used Max
Tilke's 1920s volume *Costume Patterns and Designs* as inspiration for both the
cut and decoration of her delicate chiffon smocks and kaftans (pl.118).[16]

THE BOUTIQUE REVOLUTION

The interest in second-hand clothing, particularly garments from around
1900, was an important part of this shift in aesthetic. By 1966, *Life* noted that
'English youth is deserting Carnaby Street in favour of the Portobello Road
[flea market]'.[17] About this time the shop I Was Lord Kitchener's Valet, which
specialized in second-hand military uniforms, moved from the Portobello
Road to Carnaby Street after its wares were adopted by rock stars including

Eric Clapton and Mick Jagger.[18] Second-hand uniforms, particularly dress jackets of scarlet wool with gold braid and epaulettes, were strikingly decorated yet unambiguously masculine, even if the wearer did risk being charged with impersonating a member of Her Majesty's forces.[19] In Los Angeles, Holly Harp, whose boutique catered to Hollywood actors and rock stars, described herself as 'a junk-store-aholic. I couldn't drive by one without a snake charmer coming up and grabbing me. I would just buy every hand-me-down that they had'.[20]

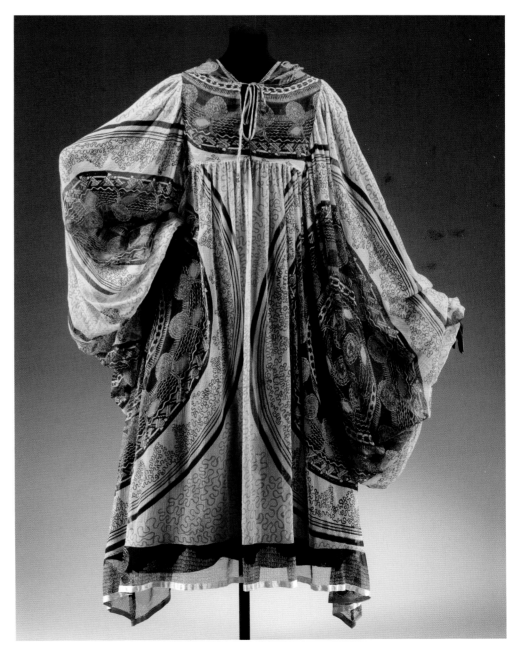

118
Zandra Rhodes, evening dress
Screen-printed silk chiffon
Britain, 1969
V&A: T.358–1974

119
**'Hippy' outfit, worn by
Shirley Abicair, 1967–9**
Hat and waistcoat:
crocheted wool, Brigitta
Bjorke, USA; blouse and
trousers: synthetic, Ossie
Clark, London; necklace:
silver and turquoise,
Morocco
V&A: T.433 to 439–1994

The cult of second-hand clothing had some paradoxical effects; on the one hand, they could be used to validate a view of clothing as art, with beautiful pieces rescued from oblivion by the connoisseur-wearer. Indeed, the façade of Granny Takes a Trip (founded 1965) bore the Wildean motto: 'One should either be a work of art or wear a work of art.'[21] On the other hand, the cheapness of second-hand garments compared to new equivalents encouraged a disposable attitude to clothes that were not seen as part of 'real' fashion. Nigel Waymouth, founder of Granny Takes a Trip, remembered that:

> we used to go down to Church Street Market and Portobello Road, collecting these old clothes, and we thought it might be a good idea to open a shop with all these things … We started off exclusively with old clothes: rather nice beaded dresses, blazers, all that sort of camp nonsense … Then we decided we'd design our own clothes … we really did pioneer … disposable clothes.[22]

The fascination with original garments from the Art Nouveau period was further piqued in 1967, when the first of a series of sales of costumes from Diaghilev's Ballets Russes was held in London. By the time of the final sale in 1973, the *Sunday Times* was suggesting that exotic costumes from *Thamar* (1912) could be wearable as well as collectable.[23] The influence of Diaghilev's aesthetic can be seen in the outfit put together by Shirley Abicair in 1967–9, orientalizing an Ossie Clark shirt and trousers by the addition of exotic necklaces and a bright crocheted waistcoat (pl.119).

Even modernist clothes were presented in ways that assimilated them to the past, in boutiques characterized in a 1966 article by 'a few pots of bright paint, some white-sprayed Victorian furniture, and grandmother's old lace curtains to run up some stock from'. An outfit illustrated in this article, by 'Annacat', consisted of an Edwardian-style lace blouse, purple velvet coat and large hat, in a photograph styled to look like a turn-of the century portrait.[24] The leader in this turn to the past was Biba, whose first shop was opened by Barbara Hulanicki on Abingdon Road, London, in 1964, moving to Kensington Church Street (1966), Kensington High Street (1969) and finally the Art Deco Derry & Toms building (again on Kensington High Street, 1973–5), by which time it was attracting 30,000 customers each Saturday. The Biba aesthetic was anti-modernist, with Hulanicki stating as early as 1965, 'I love old things … things that have lived.'[25] The styling of both the clothes and the shop interiors drew on Art Deco (and Hollywood musicals), but the overall feeling was closer to Art Nouveau in its overt sexuality and hint of transgression: 'Clothes for the sinful and *louche*: slithery gowns in glowing satins, hats with black veils, shoes stacked for sirens … makeup – chocolate and black – for vamps and vampires.'[26] The theatricality of the Biba experience, which every detail of the store from furnishings to swing tags was chosen to enhance (pl.122), responded to a view of fashion identified by the young Angela Carter in 1967:

120 *above*
Liberty & Co., 'Eustacia' textile, made up into a cocktail dress by Arnold Scaasi
Silk, block-printed
London, 1961

121 *left*
Dispo (Meyersohn & Silverstein Ltd), paper dress
Bonded cellulose fibre, screen-printed
London, 1967
V&A: T.176–1986

122
John McConnell for Pentagram, label for Biba products
Printed card
London, 1960s–70s
V&A E.3681–1983

Fashion today (real fashion, what real people wear) is a question of style ... the presentation of the self as a three-dimensional art object, to be wondered at and handled. And this involves a new attitude to the self which is thus adorned. The gaudy rags of the flower children, the element of fancy dress even in 'serious' clothes (the military look, the thirties revival) extravagant and stylised face-painting, wigs, hairpieces, amongst men the extraordinary recrudescence of the decorative moustache (and, indeed, the concept of the decorative man), fake tattooing – all these are in the nature of disguise.[27]

NEW FASHION

The paradox of the Art Nouveau revival is that it was concurrent with the development of new materials and technology normally associated with the 1960s. In fact, these technologies were an essential part of the revival, updating designs that would otherwise have been too historicist. Conversely, using designs that looked back to the past helped to alleviate the strangeness of obviously new materials. The ideal was to mediate between past and present rather than forcing the two together. In this, the Art Nouveau emphasis on surfaces rather than structures and preference for unified compositions rather than modular elements turned out to be positive assets rather than the disadvantages claimed by modernists.

For example, the starkly modern 'paper' dresses made from non-woven cellulose developed around 1966 were made from two panels with minimal shaping. It was the patterns printed on the dresses that made them desirable rather than utilitarian. Diane Meyersohn, a London designer of 'paper' dresses, used Art Nouveau motifs inspired by the V&A collections rendered in clashing shades of red and orange, green and blue, to enliven her products (pl.121).[28]

Not surprisingly, one of the firms most heavily implicated in the revival of Art Nouveau for fashion was Liberty & Co., whose company archive held thousands of key textile designs from the period 1890–1914. In 1960, under Bernard Nevill, the firm launched a 'Lotus' range, with large-scale furnishing prints from 1900 re-coloured and adapted to dress fabrics. These were an immediate success with international designers, including the American Arnold Scaasi (pl.120). Liberty's exploration of Art Nouveau designs continued throughout the 1960s, with their designer Martin Battersby creating a range in 1961 inspired by Paul Poiret.[29] Some of the prints created or revised in the 1960s, such as 'Ianthe' (1967) with its twining tendrils, are now seen as authentic Art Nouveau designs.

Art Nouveau motifs were also being used as part of a wider design vocabulary, as in the work of Emilio Pucci (1914–92), who drew on an eclectic mixture of Byzantine, Medieval, Renaissance and Aztec sources. However, the overall aesthetic of his garments, overrun with layered patterns in intense colours, is perhaps closest to Art Nouveau, and specifically to the work of the

Wiener Werkstätte in their subordination of form to surface pattern. Pucci's determined pursuit of aesthetic pleasure, and his disregard for conventions of taste or gender (trouser suits for women, flamboyant shirts and neckties for men) also aligned him to some of the dress-as-art experiments of 1900.[30]

As Carter noted, one of the most distinctive aspects of the fashions of 1966 was the opportunities they offered for 'the decorative man'. The early 1960s trend in menswear had been 'modernist' or 'mod' dressing, epitomized by slim lines, neatness and carefully selected details. When Pierre Cardin showed a controversial 'unisex' collection in 1966, it had a functionalist aesthetic based on space suits.[31] The new styles seen in London and San Francisco were quite different, embracing overt displays of a type previously regarded with suspicion as 'camp' and effeminate. This perception was accurate, as the first male boutique in London, Vince's Man's Shop (1954), had catered to overtly gay men at a time when homosexuality was still criminalized in Britain. These flamboyant clothes were re-interpreted for a more mainstream market by the entrepreneur John Stephen in a string of boutiques that opened in Carnaby Street in 1957.[32] By 1965, the traditional menswear establishments of Savile Row and Jermyn Street were adopting elements of the new styles for men, with a greater variety of shapes, colours and fabrics. In 1966 the American trade

123
Mr Fish, evening ensemble
Wool and lurex jacquard, cording and beads
London, 1970
V&A: T.705–1974

newspaper *Women's Wear Daily* stated that 'likeness in men's and women's dress . . . is terribly healthy . . . it's a symptom of liking each other. They've stopped worrying and their sick preoccupation with virility'.[33]

Independent boutique owners responded with ever more extreme styles for men: Michael Fish's shop, opened in 1966, was 'a holocaust of see-through voiles, brocades and spangles, and mini-skirts for men, blinding silks, flower-printed hats'.[34] However, these styles were presented in an environment reassuringly modelled on a traditional gentlemen's haberdasher, with oak panelling, chandeliers and suit-clad sales assistants. Fish's clothing philosophy was based on an independence that appealed to elite clients (including Old Etonians) who were 'very secure people, not the sort of man to be put off by what his wife or boss says . . . The point is, don't allow yourself to be told what to wear or how to act by others.'[35]

This attitude reached its fullest expression in a suit Fish made for himself, its jacket from wool brocaded in lurex with Art Nouveau-influenced flowers further embellished with *fin-de-siècle* cord frogging (pl.123). Fish's most notorious design, however, was probably the white tunic worn by Mick Jagger when performing at a free concert in Hyde Park, London, in 1969. This was described in the press as a 'little girl's white party frock'.[36] In addition to gathering attention for both designers and wearers, the extremes of androgynous style defused opposition to more discreet initiatives such as shirts and ties made up in densely patterned fabrics to offset plain wool suits (pl.125). By 1970, wide 'Kipper' ties in Art Nouveau revival prints were being produced by firms from Liberty & Co. (pl.124) to Pucci of Florence.

The Art Nouveau revival opened up contrasting possibilities in fashion. It provided an alternative model of gender definition, with men preening peacock-like in flamboyant fabrics, while women covered themselves in trailing draperies. The Art Nouveau emphasis on pattern and surface decoration provided a relief from the solid colours and flat textures of

124
Men's ties
Printed silk
London, c.1965–70
From left: Liberty,
V&A: T.183-1978,
V&A: T.198-1979,
V&A: T.199-1979; John
Michael, V&A: T.202-1979;
Hung on You,
V&A: T.314-1979; Mr Fish,
V&A: T.706-1974; Hayward,
V&A: T.365-1979

modernist garments, and challenged conventional notions of taste and decorum. The historical basis of the revival both legitimated and ironized some of its more unconventional initiatives, such as the jackets made from iconic William Morris furnishing textiles by Granny Takes a Trip.[37] Most radical, however, was the do-it-yourself nature of the Art Nouveau revival, based on garments sourced from the past or from distant cultures.

Originating in Haight Ashbury and the Portobello Road, the style flowed upwards into Paris couture, challenging the top-down ethos of conventional fashion prediction. Indeed, some of the items produced by small boutiques had more claim to exclusivity than those from conventional couture houses. The menswear boutique 'Hung on You' offered leather garments made to order by Mirandi Babitz and Clem Floyd. For the interior designer David Mlinaric, the duo produced a tunic with his choice of motif worked in a painstaking inlay technique rather than the more usual appliqué (pl.126). The makers' insistence on the highest standards and refusal to license designs took them back to the

125
Tommy Nutter, suit
Cream wool
London, 1973
V&A: T.152 to 154–1995
Take Six, shirt
Printed wool mix
London, c.1970
V&A: T.107–1985

Mirandi Babitz and Clem Floyd for Hung on You, leather jacket with intarsia
London, 1967
V&A T.313–1979

practices of *fin-de-siècle* couture – or even beyond them, since Worth and Paquin had gladly embraced diffusion ranges and product licensing.

The varied interpretations of the *fin de siècle* also pointed forwards to Ted Polhemus's identification of late twentieth-century design as a 'supermarket of styles' in which almost anything could be justified. Ossie Clark's garments were made in softly draping fabrics with Celia Birtwell prints that referenced the motifs of the Wiener Werkstätte and Paul Poiret. In 1969 Clark's culotte dress was photographed against a biplane that placed it implicitly in the Wright Brothers era, around 1910 (pl.128). The draped gowns and cloaks produced by Gnyuki Torimaru (Yuki) in the 1970s showed their debt to Art Nouveau fashion in fluid lines and simple construction reminiscent of the chemise dresses of Poiret and the pleated 'chitons' of Fortuny (pl.127). Perhaps most profoundly, these garments prioritized the aesthetic judgement of the wearer over the observance of fashion cycles. Unlike Modernism, which searched for rational solutions to the problems of living, Art Nouveau retained an element of fantasy. Art Nouveau fashion allowed the wearer to play with styles from different times and cultures – or to present the body as a walking work of art. It is this fluidity, and this sense of aesthetic potential, that present the lasting legacy of Art Nouveau fashion.

127 *left*
Yuki evening cloak
Rayon jersey and organdie
London, 1977
V&A: T.1-1979

128 *opposite*
Jim Lee, Ossie Clark
Plane Crash, 1969
Britain, 1969
V&A: E.14-2006

Introduction

1 'L'Art Nouveau: What it is and what is thought of it', in Howard, *Art Nouveau*, p.1
2 Howard, p.34
3 *Journal des arts décoratifs* (1892), in Escritt, *Art Nouveau*, p.88
4 Cornu, 'L'Art de la robe', p.116 (author translation)
5 Taylor, 'Art and Crafts Dress', in Livingstone and Parry (eds), *International Arts and Crafts*, pp.224–7
6 Cornu, p.102 (author translation)
7 Introduction, *Les Toilettes de la collectivité de la Couture* (1900)
8 Muthesius, 'The English House' (1904), cited in Burkhauser (ed.), *Glasgow Girls*, pp.50–5 (1993)
9 'Modern Decorative Art in Glasgow', *The Studio* (1906), cited in Burkhauser, p.54
10 Taylor, 'Why the Absence of Fashionable Dress…', from *Fashion Theory*, vol. 6/1, pp.311–21 (2002)
11 All these firms are named in *Les Toilettes de la collectivité de la Couture* (1900); see also Françoise Tétart-Vittu, 'The Origins of Haute Couture', in Saillard and Zazzo (eds), *Paris Haute Couture*, pp.18–21
12 Rose, 'Advertising Ready-Made Style', from *Textile History*, vol. 40, no. 2, pp.185–201 (November 2009)
13 Breward, *The Hidden Consumer*, Chapter 6

Chapter 1

1 Chrisman-Campbell, 'Rose Bertin'
2 Coleman, *Opulent Era*, p.21; Tétart-Vittu, 'The Origins of Haute Couture'
3 Jungbluth, *Les Créateurs*
4 Coleman, p.21
5 Perrot, *Fashioning the Bourgeoisie*, Chapter V, pp.58–79; Adburgham, *Shops and Shopping*, Chapter XIII
6 Adburgham, p.65. The Parisian couturiers Aine-Montaillé had also started by selling mourning; Musée de la Mode et du Costume, *Femmes fin de siècle*, p.186
7 For example 'John Noble's Novelties', 1895, reproduced in facsimile as pp.72–96 in Rose and Richmond (eds), *Clothing, Society and Culture*, vol. I
8 Bass-Krueger, 'From the "union parfaite" . . . ', p.32
9 C.F. Worth pioneered bias-cut dresses with a single seam spiralling from shoulder to hip in 1891, but these were not generally adopted; De Marly, *Worth*, pp.192–4
10 Interview with C.F. Worth, 1871, in Coleman, p.18

11 Coleman, p.108. French trademark regulations had been expanded to cover the fashion trades in 1884; Musée de la Mode et du Costume, p.186
12 Coleman, pp.36–8
13 Coleman, p.16
14 Coleman, p.15
15 Coleman, pp.20–23
16 Reeder, 'Paquin, Jeanne'
17 Jean Béraud, *Sortie des ouvrières de la maison Paquin, rue de la Paix* (c.1900); Musée Carnavalet, Paris P1662
18 Lehmann, 'Tigersprung: Fashioning History'; see also catalogue number 4 in Musée Historique des Tissus, *Paquin*, p.20
19 Metropolitan Museum of Art C.I.48.70.1
20 Metropolitan Museum of Art 1979.346.27. This may be based on the design illustrated as catalogue number 6 in Musée Historique des Tissus, *Paquin*, p.21
21 For example, a dress and coat in purple cloth, Winter 1908 collection, V&A: E.1915–1957 and V&A: E.1916–1957 in Volume 34 of the Paquin archive
22 Reeder
23 Cited in Troy, *Couture Culture*, p.129
24 Sorkin, 'Lucile'
25 V&A: T.89A–1986, reproduced in facsimile in Mendes and de la Haye, *Lucile Ltd*
26 Mendes and de la Haye, pp.65, 171
27 Sorkin
28 For Lucile's tailoring, see V&A: T.36–1960 and V&A: T.41–1960, worn by Heather Firbank. For Lucile's work in movies, see Finamore, *Hollywood Before Glamour*, pp.74–106
29 See the slightly later example, 'Reverend', 1905, Palais Galliera 1963.30.3
30 Cartoon, 'The Pioneer' Punch, 15 March 1911, illustrated in Walkley, *The Way to Wear 'Em*, p.121
31 'The appanage of the really chic woman', *Illustrated London News*, February 1911
32 Davis, *Ballets Russes Style*, pp.129–38
33 Davis, *Classic Chic*, p.44
34 'Mrs Asquith and French dresses', *The Times* (1909)
35 Chicago History Museum, 1958.182, illustrated in Koda and Bolton, *Poiret*, pp.102–3; Museum of the Fashion Institute of Technology, New York, P81.8.1
36 Troy, *Couture Culture*, pp.211–50; 'Newest "Bakst Minaret"', *Evening Herald* (1914)

37 Coleman, *Age of Opulence*, p.37; de la Haye, 'Carresaute, an Evening Gown', in Mendes and de la Haye, *Lucile*, pp.77–81
38 This project was influenced by Poiret's 1910 visit to the Wiener Werkstätte, discussed in Chapter 6
39 Koda and Bolton, pp.66–9
40 The scrolled fabric commissioned by Worth is found in three extant examples: one in black on white, MMA 1976.258.1; one in pale green, MMA 57.17.8; and one in pink on white, Chicago History Museum 1959.190. See Coleman, *Opulent Era*, pp.78–9

Chapter 2

1 Escritt, *Art Nouveau*, p.93
2 Calouste Gulbenkian Museum, Lisbon, purchased by the founder from Lalique, 1903; Becker, *Jewellery of René Lalique*, no. 87
3 Howard, *Art Nouveau*, p.20
4 Ockman and Silver (eds), *Sarah Bernhardt*, p.13. Lalique had designed a snake tiara for Bernhardt in *Theodora*, 1898
5 Zapata, *The Jewelry and Enamels*, pp.21–2 and figure 2; Tiffany, *Tiffany & Co. Exhibit, Paris Exposition 1900*
6 Zapata, pp.76–80
7 Zapata, p.97
8 Illustrated in Becker, pp.28–9
9 Becker, no. 144
10 Becker, p.25
11 Contemporary critics noted that the use of semi-precious materials was linked to greater experimentation in jewellery; Vallance, 'British Jewellery and Fans' (1902), p.42
12 Calloway, 'Metalwork', in Calloway (ed.), *Liberty of London*, pp.86–99
13 Escritt, p.331
14 Cited in Escritt, p.316
15 Vallance, p.50
16 Musée Historique des Tissus, *Paquin*, p.88
17 Alexander, *Advertising Fans*
18 Koda and Bolton, *Poiret*, pp.104–5
19 Sometimes spelled Yantourney; a trunk of shoes made by him for Rita de Acosta Lydig is in the Metropolitan Museum, C.I.53.76.1a,b–12a,b
20 Font, 'Chanel'
21 There was a near-riot when supplies of free hats fell short; Majer (ed.), *Staging Fashion*, pp.132–6
22 A Fabergé parasol set with diamonds, V&A: T.39–1958, is illustrated in Wilcox and Lister (eds), *V&A Gallery of Fashion*, p.75
23 Silver, 'Forbidden Fruits: The Perfumes of Rosine', in Koda and Bolton, pp.47–51
24 Illustrated in Austrian Ministry, *Exhibition of Professional Schools*, pp.29, 31

Chapter 3

1 Breward, 'Patterns of Respectability'; Beetham, *A Magazine of Her Own*

2 These categories were sometimes blurred by the provision of additional pattern diagrams, cut paper patterns, and fashion plates for use by professionals, on subscription only; French magazines offered up to five different subscriptions with and without patterns. See Annie Barbera, 'Des journaux et des modes', pp.103–18, in Musée de la Mode et du Costume, *Femmes fin de siècle*

3 Rose and Richmond (eds), *Clothing, Society and Culture*, vol.1, *Buying and Selling Clothes*, pp.141–62

4 Rose and Richmond (eds), *Clothing, Society and Culture,* vol.2, *Abuses and Reforms*, pp.397–416

5 Mackrell, *Art and Fashion*, p.114; Taylor, 'Why the Absence of Fashionable Dress . . .', pp.314–8; Mulvagh, *Vogue History*, pp.12–31

6 De Marly, *History of Haute Couture*, p.113

7 Davis, *Classic Chic*, pp.16–18, 48–92; Majer (ed.), *Staging Fashion*

8 Rose and Richmond (eds), vol.1, pp.1–24

9 Verhagen, 'The poster in *fin-de-siècle* Paris'

10 Breward, *The Hidden Consumer*, pp.111–21

11 Rappaport, *Shopping for Pleasure*, pp.142–77 and pp.215–22

12 Rose and Richmond (eds), vol.1; 'Harris and Sheldon Catalogue 1911', pp.191–202

13 Charlotte Piot, 'The Dressmaker's Mannequin', in Saillard and Zazzo (eds), *Paris Haute Couture*, pp.58–61

14 Kaplan and Stowell, *Theatre and Fashion*, pp.115–51

15 William de Gregorio, 'Jane Hading', in Majer (ed.), pp.92–125

16 Redfern advertisement, *The Times*, Monday, 6 July 1908, p.12

17 Sheila Stowell, 'Lucile and the Theatricalization of Fashion', in Majer, (ed.), pp.60–75

18 de Gregorio, in Majer (ed.), p.119

19 Kaplan and Stowell, pp.45, 71–81; the costumes for Eliza Doolittle were designed by Madame Handley Seymour; see plate 11

20 Musée Historique des Tissus, *Paquin*, image on p.79

21 Galtier, 'Répétition générale au Vaudeville: Rue de la Paix', *Excelsior* (Paris), p.7, 22 January 1912, in Troy, *Couture Culture*, p.133

22 Musée Historique des Tissus, p.88

23 Troy, pp.112–8

24 Koda and Bolton, *Poiret*, images on pp.23 and 28

25 Finamore, *Hollywood Before Glamour*, pp.37–41; image on p.40

26 Mendes and de la Haye, *Lucile Ltd,* pp.32–9

27 Levitt, *Fashion in Photographs*

28 Majer, 'Staging Fashion, 1880–1920', in Majer (ed.), *Staging Fashion*, pp.18–47

29 Finamore, Chapter 4

30 Evans, 'Enchanted Spectacle', p.285

31 Desmond, 'London Life'

32 Musée Historique des Tissus, p.87

33 The London department store Peter Robinson presented one of these in 1904; Evans, p.283

34 Finamore, 'Fashion Shows'; Font, 'International couture', p.34

35 Mendes, 'Most Bewitching gowns . . . 1890–1905', in Mendes and de la Haye, pp.16–29

36 Marie Corelli review of Lucile show in *Bystander*, 1904, cited in Majer (ed.), pp.66–8

37 Keenan, *The Women We Wanted to Look Like*, pp.111–13; Mendes and de la Haye, pp.184–6. However, mannequins for other houses remained anonymous; Taylor, 'Marguerite Shoobert'

38 Cunningham, *Reforming Women's Fashion*, p.208; Rose and Richmond (eds), vol.2, pp.285–300

39 Cunningham, pp.61–5

40 Wade, *A Week at the Fair*, p.244

41 Silverman, *Art Nouveau*, p.291

42 Meier-Graefe, *Die Weltanstellung in Paris 1900*, p.132

43 'The Paris Exhibition', *Morning Post*, 3 May 1900, p.5

44 'Earl's Court Exhibition', *The Times*, 9 June 1902, p.7

45 Font, 'International couture', p.32

46 Austrian Ministry for Public Instruction, *Exhibition of Professional Schools for Arts and Crafts*, 1904

47 Mrs Humphry (of *Truth*), 'Fashion Exhibits', p.218

48 'The Franco-British Exhibition', *The Times*, 6 June 1908, p.4

49 'Franco-British Exhibition – Furs and Feathers', *The Times*, 22 June 1908, p.16

50 Troy, pp.148–9

Chapter 4

1 Nadine Bosc, 'The Couturier and His Clients in the Second Half of the Nineteenth Century', in Saillard and Zazzo (eds), *Paris Haute Couture*, pp.22–5

2 If a husband accompanied his wife shopping, he would be expected to pay the bill with his own money, rather than from his wife's limited dress allowance, and if he refused the retailer could take him to court. Rappaport, *Shopping for Pleasure,* Women in the Making of London's West End, pp.48–73 and especially p.69

3 Bosc, p.24

4 Coleman, *Opulent Era*, p.95

5 *Vogue*, 10 August 1893, in Coleman, p.90

6 Cited in Coleman, p.95

7 De Marly, *Worth*, pp.154–5

8 Strasdin, 'Empire Dressing', p.162

9 North, 'John Redfern and Sons', p.157; Rose, 'What was uniform'

10 This was three times the typical cost for a court dress, reflecting the unique nature of the commission; Strasdin, p.162

11 Strasdin, pp.157–8

12 Queen Alexandra to Mary Curzon, 1901; cited in Strasdin, p.165

13 Illustrated in Metropolitan Museum, *Wild: Fashion Untamed*, p.106

14 Thomas, 'Embodying Imperial Spectacle', p.384

15 Mrs M.E.W. Sherwood, *The American Code of Manners* (1884), in Coleman, p.89

16 Bosc, p.23

17 Coleman, p.89

18 Shaw, *World's Fair Notes*, p.61

19 Weimann, *The Fair Women*, p.12

20 Chicago History Museum, www.digitalcollection. chicagohistory.org

21 In the 1920s, Grigsby wore a striking orange, knee-length dance dress with fringed skirts, suggesting the movement of the Charleston; V&A: T.139–1967

22 Damien Delille, 'The Client, the Couturier, and the Flower: Interweaving Inspirations', in Saillard and Zazzo (eds), *Paris Haute Couture*, pp.54–7

23 Steele, *Paris Fashion: A Cultural History*, pp.212–14

24 Coleman, p.101

25 Beaton, *The Glass of Fashion*, p.126

26 Beaton, p.124

27 Beaton, pp.126–7

28 Mrs Drummond left the considerable sum of £9,000 when she died in 1917; thanks to Jenny Lister of the V&A for this information

29 V&A: T.71–1960

30 Stewart, 'Copying and copyrighting', p.106

31 Davis, *Classic Chic*, pp.164–5

Chapter 5

1 Cunningham, *Reforming Women's Fashion*, pp.112–25; Rose and Richmond (eds), *Clothing, Society and Culture*, vol.2, pp.xiv–xvi, 285–299; Stewart and Janovicek, 'Slimming the Female Body'

2 Poiret, *King of Fashion*, p.36

3 Steele, *The Corset*, pp.80–85

4 Poiret, p.36

5 Thanks to Sue Ralph for sharing her research on Margaine-Lacroix
6 Anderson, 'This Sporting Cloth'
7 McGurn, On Your Bicycle, pp.100–22
8 'The Viscountess and the Pub Landlady' in Rose and Richmond (eds), Clothing, Society and Culture, vol. III, pp.319–40
9 Williams, 'Aquadynamics'
10 Wood, Art Nouveau and the Erotic, pp.50–59
11 Wood
12 Crawford, 'Beardsley'; Edwards, 'Wilde'
13 Proust, Within a Budding Grove, pp.569–70, in Steele, Paris Fashion, p.211
14 Breward, The Hidden Consumer, pp.230–45
15 Poiret, p.24
16 Ockman and Silver, Sarah Bernhardt, pp.100, 141–2
17 Brandon, Being Divine, figures 7–9
18 Ockman and Silver, p.13
19 Pritchard, Diaghilev, pp.49–55
20 Current and Current, Loïe Fuller, p.99
21 Current and Current, pp.343–51
22 Garelick, Electric Salome, p.78
23 Cunningham, pp.213–15
24 Davis, Classic Chic, pp.16–21
25 Pritchard, pp.220–1
26 Troy, Couture Culture, pp.116–22
27 Marlis Schweitzer, 'Stylish Effervescence: Burke and the Rise of the Fashionable Broadway Star', in Majer (ed.), pp.77–90

Chapter 6

1 Taylor, 'Why the Absence of Fashionable Dress…'
2 Emmanuelle Serrière, 'The Invention of the Label', in Saillard and Zazzo (eds), Paris Haute Couture, pp.26–9
3 Tétart-Vittu, 'The Origins of Haute Couture'
4 Troy, Couture Culture, pp.245–64; Stewart, 'Copying and Copyrighting', p.109. A 1917 court case against copyists, by Boué Soeurs, only succeeded because deception was involved; Font, 'International Couture', p.39
5 Davis, Classic Chic, pp.115–16; Gee and Grimaud, 'Doucet'
6 Silverman, Fin de Siècle, p.275
7 Conder's fans are illustrated in Vallance, 'British Jewellery', pp.51 and 56; several examples survive in the collections of Tate Britain (N04243 and N03194)
8 Loos, 'Men's Fashion', in Spoken into the Void, p.11
9 Adburgham, Liberty's, pp.51–8
10 Adburgham, p.88; Liberty catalogues from 1886 on are held in the NAL
11 Lavallée, 'Art Nouveau'
12 Silverman, p.272

13 Illustrated in Fahr-Becker, Art Nouveau, p.156
14 Van de Velde, Kunstgewerbliche Leienpredigten (Leipzig, 1902), in Fahr-Becker, Wiener Werkstaette, p.21
15 Burkhauser, p.54
16 Bird, 'Women and Art Education' in Burkhauser, Glasgow Girls, pp.71–5
17 See Vallance, 'British Jewellery and Fans' for examples by Glasgow designers including Mackintosh
18 Muther, cited on p.121 in Timothy Neat, 'Tinker, Tailor, Soldier, Sailor: Margaret Macdonald and the Principle of Choice', in Burkhauser, Glasgow Girls, pp.117–21
19 Houze, 'From Wiener Kunst im Hause'
20 Prossinger, 'Vienna', in Makela et al, 'Secession'
21 Gronberg, Vienna: City of Modernity, 1890–1914, pp.138–42
22 Deutsche Kunst und Dekoration, vol. 19; see Gronberg, pp.126–8
23 Völker, Textiles of the Wiener Werkstätte, pp.43–8
24 Fahr-Becker, Wiener Werkstaette, p.62
25 Zuckerkandel, cited in Mackrell, Art and Fashion, p.124
26 'Omega Workshops'
27 Hess, 'The Lure of Vienna: Poiret and the Wiener Werkstätte', in Koda and Bolton, Poiret, pp.39–40
28 Pérez-Tibi, 'Dufy'
29 Troy, pp.137–40; Davis, Ballets Russes Style, pp.172–80
30 Troy, pp.152–5
31 Damase, Sonia Delaunay

Chapter 7

1 Tilburg, 'Mimi Pinson Goes to War'
2 For social sanctions against spending on fashion during the First World War, see Ugolini, Men and Menswear, Chapter 6
3 Bass-Krueger, 'From the "union parfaite"…'
4 Finamore, Hollywood Before Glamour, pp.45–73
5 Davis, Classic Chic, p.164
6 Morton Shand, letter to William Davidson, cited in Burkhauser, 'Introduction', p.23
7 Phillipe Thiébaut, 'Historique', in Thiébaut (ed.), Art Nouveau Revival, pp.21–47
8 Thiébaut, 'Historique', p.24
9 Thiébaut, 'Historique', p.22
10 Guffey, Retro: The Culture of Revival, pp.49–52
11 Melly, Revolt into Style: The Pop Arts (London, 1971), cited in Guffey, p.52
12 Guffey, p.53
13 Guffey, p.11
14 Phillipe Thiébaut, 'Graphique', in Thiébaut (ed.), Art Nouveau Revival, pp.105–67

15 Time (1967), cited in Guffey, p.63
16 Rhodes, The Art of Zandra Rhodes, p.37
17 Lobenthal, Radical Rags, p.31
18 Orbach, 'Interview'
19 Such a court case is mentioned in 'On Parade in Portobello Road', The Times, 23 September 1966
20 Lobenthal, Radical Rags, p.127
21 Sandbrook, White Heat, p.427
22 Nigel Waymouth on the origins of 'Granny Takes a Trip', in Green, All Dressed Up, pp.80–1
23 Pritchard, 'Diaghilev Under the Hammer', in Pritchard (ed.), Diaghilev, pp.166–7
24 Glynn, 'Boutiques – or what you will'
25 Barbara Hulanicki (1965), quoted in Sandbrook, White Heat, p.428
26 Alexandra Pringle, 'Chelsea Girl', in Maitland, I Believe in Yesterday, pp.35–40
27 Carter, 'Notes for a Theory of Sixties Style', New Society (1967), cited in Caroline Evans, 'Postwar Poses: 1955–75' in Breward, Ehrman and Evans, London Look, pp.117–38, on p.133
28 Thanks to Jenny Lister for this information
29 Adburgham, Liberty's, p.154; Buruma, Liberty & Co. in the Fifties and Sixties, pp.93–112
30 Biennale di Firenze, Emilio Pucci
31 Jenny Lister, 'Kaleidoscope: Fashion in Sixties London', in Breward et al., Swinging Sixties, pp.22–41
32 Fogg, Boutique, pp.67–75
33 Lobenthal, Radical Rags, p.155
34 Nik Cohn, cited in Fogg, p.70
35 Lobenthal, pp.146–9
36 Lobenthal, p.204
37 Fogg, p.66

BIBLIOGRAPHY

Adburgham, Alison, *Liberty's: A Biography of A Shop* (London: George Allen & Unwin, 1975)
—— *Shops and Shopping 1800–1914* (London: Barrie and Jenkins, 1989)
Alexander, Hélène, *Advertising Fans* (London: The Fan Museum, 2005)
Anderson, Fiona, 'This Sporting Cloth: Tweed, Gender and Fashion 1860–1900', *Textile History*, 37:2 (2006)
Bass-Krueger, Maude, 'From the "*union parfaite*" to the "*union brisée*": the French Couture Industry and the midinettes during the Great War', *Costume*, vol. 47, no.1 (January 2013)
Beaton, Cecil, *The Glass of Fashion* (London: Weidenfeld & Nicolson, 1954)
Becker, Vivienne, *The Jewellery of René Lalique* (London: Goldsmiths' Company, 1987)
Beetham, Margaret, *A Magazine of Her Own: Domesticity and Desire in the Woman's Magazine,* 1800–1914 (London: Routledge, 1996)
Biennale di Firenze, *Emilio Pucci* (Florence, 1996)
Brandon, Ruth, *Being Divine: A Biography of Sarah Bernhardt* (London: Secker & Warburg, 1991)
—— *The Dollar Princesses: The American Invasion of the European Aristocracy 1870–1914* (London: Weidenfeld and Nicolson, 1980)
Breward, Christopher, 'Patterns of Respectability: Publishing, Home Sewing and the Dynamics of Class and Gender 1870–1914' in Burman, Barbara (ed.), *The Culture of Sewing: Gender, Consumption and Home Dressmaking* (Oxford: Berg, 1999)
—— *The Hidden Consumer: Masculinities, Fashion and City Life 1860–1914* (Manchester: Manchester University Press, 1999)
—— Ehrman, Edwina and Evans, Caroline, *The London Look: Fashion from Street to Catwalk* (New Haven and London: Yale University Press, 2004)
—— Gilbert, David and Lister, Jenny, *Swinging Sixties: Fashion in London and Beyond* (London: V&A, 2006)
Burkhauser, Jude (ed.), *The Glasgow Girls: Women in Art and Design, 1880–1920* (Edinburgh: Canongate Press, 1993)
Buruma, Anna, *Liberty & Co. in the Fifties and Sixties: A Taste for Design* (Woodbridge, Suffolk: ACC Editions, 2009)
Calloway, Stephen (ed.), *Liberty of London: Masters of Style and Decoration* (London: Thames & Hudson, 1992)

Chrisman-Campbell, Kimberly, 'Rose Bertin', *The Berg Fashion Library*, 2005; web: 28 October 2013, www.bergfashionlibrary.com
Coleman, Elizabeth Ann, *The Opulent Era: Fashions of Worth, Doucet and Pingat* (London: Thames & Hudson and the Brooklyn Museum, 1989)
Crawford, Alan, 'Beardsley, Aubrey Vincent (1872–1898)' in *Oxford Dictionary of National Biography* (Oxford: Oxford University Press, 2004)
Cunningham, Patricia, *Reforming Women's Fashion 1850–1920, Politics, Health and Art* (Kent, OH: Kent State University Press, 2003)
Current, Richard Nelson and Current, Marcia Ewing, *Loïe Fuller: Goddess of Light* (Boston: Northeastern University Press, 1997)
Damase, Jacques, *Sonia Delaunay: Fashion and Fabrics* (London: Thames & Hudson, 1991)
Davis, Mary E., *Ballets Russes Style, Diaghilev's Dancers and Paris Fashion* (London: Reaktion, 2010)
—— *Classic Chic: Music, Fashion and Modernism* (Berkeley: University of California Press, 2006)
de la Haye, Amy and Dingwall, Cathy (eds), *Surfers Soulies Skinheads and Skaters: Subcultural Style from the Forties to the Nineties* (London: V&A, 1996)
—— and Mendes, Valerie D., *The House of Worth: Portrait of an Archive* (London: V&A, 2014)
De Marly, Diana, *The History of Haute Couture 1850–1950* (London: B.T. Batsford Ltd, 1980)
—— *Worth: Father of Haute Couture* (London: Elm Tree Books, 1980)
Dudley Edwards, Owen, 'Wilde, Oscar Fingal O'Flahertie Wills (1854–1900)' in *Oxford Dictionary of National Biography* (Oxford: Oxford University Press, 2004); online edn, January 2010
Escritt, Stephen, *Art Nouveau* (London: Phaidon, 2000)
Evans, Caroline, 'The Enchanted Spectacle', *Fashion Theory*, vol. 5/3 (2001)
Fahr-Becker, Gabriele, *Wiener Werkstaette 1903–1932* (Koln: Benedikt Taschen, 1995)
—— *Art Nouveau* (Potsdam: h.f. ullmann, 2007)
Finamore, Michelle Tolini, *Hollywood Before Glamour: Fashion in American Silent Film* (New York/London: St Martin's Press/Palgrave Macmillan, 2013)
—— 'Fashion Shows', *The Berg Fashion Library*, 2005; web: 2 September 2013, www.bergfashionlibrary.com

Fogg, Marnie, *Boutique: A '60s Cultural Phenomenon* (London: Mitchell Beazley, 2003)
Font, Lourdes M., 'Chanel, Coco [Gabrielle Bonheur]', *Grove Art Online. Oxford Art Online.* Oxford University Press; web: 31 July 2013, www.oxfordartonline.com
—— 'International Couture: The Opportunities and Challenges of Expansion, 1880–1920', *Business History*, 54:1 (2012)
Garelick, Rhonda K., *Electric Salome: Loïe Fuller's Performance of Modernism* (Princeton: Princeton University Press, 2007)
Gee, Malcolm and Grimaud, Pamela Elizabeth, 'Doucet, Jacques', *Grove Art Online. Oxford Art Online.* Oxford University Press; web: 31 July 2013, www.oxfordartonline.com
Green, Jonathan, *All Dressed Up: The Sixties and the Counterculture* (London: Pimlico, 1999)
Greenhalgh, Paul, *Ephemeral Vistas: The Expositions Universelles, Great Exhibitions and World's Fairs, 1851–1939* (Manchester: Manchester University Press, 1988)
—— (ed.), *Art Nouveau: 1890–1914* (London: V&A, 2000)
Gronberg, Tag, *Vienna: City of Modernity, 1890–1914* (Oxford: Peter Lang, 2007)
Guffey, Elizabeth E., *Retro: The Culture of Revival* (London: Reaktion, 2006)
Houze, Rebecca, 'From Wiener Kunst im Hause to the Wiener Werkstätte: Marketing Domesticity with Fashionable Interior Design', *Design Issues*, vol. 18, no. 1 (Winter 2002)
Howard, Jeremy, *Art Nouveau: International and National Styles in Europe* (Manchester: Manchester University Press, 1996)
Jobling, Paul and Crowley, David, *Graphic Design: Reproduction and Representation since 1800* (Manchester: Manchester University Press, 1996)
Kaplan, Joel and Stowell, Sheila, *Theatre and Fashion: Oscar Wilde to the Suffragettes* (Cambridge: Cambridge University Press, 1994)
Keenan, Brigid, *The Women We Wanted to Look Like* (New York: St Martin's Press, 1978)
Koda, Harold and Bolton, Andrew (eds), *Poiret* (New York: Metropolitan Museum of Art/New Haven: Yale University Press, 2007)
Lavallée, Michèle, 'Art Nouveau', *Grove Art Online. Oxford Art Online.* Oxford University Press; web: 22 August 2013, www.oxfordartonline.com

Lehmann, Ulrich, 'Tigersprung: Fashioning History', *Fashion Theory: The Journal of Dress, Body & Culture*, vol. 3, no. 3 (August 1999)

Levitt, Sarah, *Fashion in Photographs 1880–1900* (London: B.T. Batsford Ltd in association with the National Portrait Gallery, 1991)

Livingstone, Karen and Parry, Linda (eds), *International Arts and Crafts* (London: V&A, 2005)

Lobenthal, Joel, *Radical Rags: Fashion of the Sixties* (New York: Abbeville, 1990)

Lynn, Eleri, *Underwear: Fashion in Detail* (London: V&A, 2010)

McGurn, James, *On Your Bicycle: An Illustrated History of Cycling* (London: John Murray, 1987)

Mackrell, Alice, *Art and Fashion* (London: Batsford, 2004)

Maitland, Sara, *I Believe in Yesterday* (London: Virago, 1988)

Majer, Michele (ed.), *Staging Fashion 1880–1920: Jane Hading, Lily Elsie, Billie Burke* (New York: Bard Graduate Center, 2012)

Makela, Maria, et al., 'Secession', *Grove Art Online. Oxford Art Online.* Oxford University Press; web: 31 July 2013, www.oxfordartonline.com

Mendes, Valerie and de la Haye, Amy, *Lucile Ltd: London, Paris, New York and Chicago 1890s–1930s* (London: V&A, 2009)

Metropolitan Museum of Art, *Wild: Fashion Untamed* (New York: Metropolitan Museum of Art, 2004)

Mulvagh, Jane, *Vogue History of 20th Century Fashion* (London: Bloomsbury Books, 1988)

Musée de la Mode et du Costume Palais Galliera, *Femmes fin de siècle 1885–1895* (Paris: Éditions Paris-Musées, 1990)

Musée Historique des Tissus, Lyon, *Paquin, une rétrospective de 60 ans de haute couture* (Lyon: Musée Historique des Tissus, 1989)

North, Susan, 'John Redfern and Sons, 1847–1892', *Costume*, vol. 42 (2008)

Ockman, Carol and Silver, Kenneth E. (eds), *Sarah Bernhardt: The Art of High Drama* (New York/New Haven and London: The Jewish Museum/Yale University Press, 2005)

'Omega Workshops', *Grove Art Online. Oxford Art Online.* Oxford University Press; web: 3 September 2013, www.oxfordartonline.com

Orbach, Robert, 'Interview with the V&A' (2006), www.vam.ac.uk/content/articles/i/robert-orbach/

Pérez-Tibi, Dora, 'Dufy, Raoul', *Grove Art Online. Oxford Art Online.* Oxford University Press; web: 12 July 2013, www.oxfordartonline.com

—— and Stewart, Kristen E., 'Poiret, Paul', *Grove Art Online. Oxford Art Online.* Oxford University Press; web: 12 July 2013, www.oxfordartonline.com

Perrot, Phillipe, *Fashioning the Bourgeoisie: A History of Clothing in the Nineteenth Century* (Princeton, NJ: Princeton University Press, 1994)

Pritchard, Jane (ed.), *Diaghilev and the Golden Age of the Ballets Russes 1909–1929* (London: V&A, 2010)

Rappaport, Erika, *Shopping for Pleasure: Women in the Making of London's West End* (Princeton, NJ: Princeton University Press, 2000)

Reeder, Jan Glier, 'Paquin, Jeanne', *Grove Art Online. Oxford Art Online.* Oxford University Press; web: 11 July 2013

Rheims, Maurice, *L'Objet 1900* (Paris: Arts et Métiers Graphiques, 1964)

—— *L'Art 1900 ou le Style Jules Verne* (Paris: Arts et Métiers Graphiques, 1965)

Rhodes, Zandra and Knight, Anne, *The Art of Zandra Rhodes* (London: Jonathan Cape, 1984)

Rose, Clare, 'Advertising Ready-Made Style: The Evidence of the Stationers' Hall Archive', *Textile History*, vol. 40/2 (2009)

Rose, Clare, 'What was uniform about the *fin-de-siècle* sailor suit?', *Journal of Design History*, 24/2 (2011)

—— and Richmond, Vivienne (eds), *Clothing, Society and Culture* (London: Pickering & Chatto, 2011); Volume 1, *Buying and Selling Clothes*; Volume 2, *Abuses and Reforms*

Saillard, Olivier and Zazzo, Anne (eds), *Paris Haute Couture* (Paris: Flammarion, 2013)

Sandbrook, Dominic, *White Heat: A History of Britain in the Swinging Sixties* (London: Abacus, 2007)

Silverman, Debora A., *Art Nouveau in Fin-de-siècle France: Politics, Psychology and Style* (Berkeley, CA: University of California Press, 1989)

Slevin, Tom, 'Sonia Delaunay's Robe Simultané: Modernity, Fashion, and Transmediality', *Fashion Theory*, vol. 17, issue 1 (2013)

Sorkin, Molly, 'Lucile', *Grove Art Online. Oxford Art Online.* Oxford University Press; web: 11 July 2013, www.oxfordartonline.com

Steele, Valerie, *Paris Fashion: A Cultural History* (New York: Oxford University Press, 1988)

—— *The Corset: A Cultural History* (New Haven, CT; London: Yale University Press, 2001)

Stewart, Mary Lynn, 'Copying and Copyrighting Haute Couture: Democratizing Fashion, 1900–1930s', *French Historical Studies*, vol. 28/1 (Winter 2005)

—— and Janovicek, Nancy, 'Slimming the Female Body? Re-evaluating Dress, Corsets, and Physical Culture in France, 1890s–1930s', *Fashion Theory*, 5/2 (2001), pp.173–94

Strasdin, Kate, 'Empire Dressing – The Design and Realization of Queen Alexandra's Coronation Gown', *Journal of Design History*, vol. 25/2 (2012)

—— 'Fashioning Alexandra: A Royal Approach to Style 1863–1910', *Costume*, vol. 47/2 (2013)

Taylor, Lou, 'Marguerite Shoobert, London fashion model 1906–1917', *Costume*, vol. 17 (1983)

—— 'Why the Absence of Fashionable Dress in the Victoria and Albert Museum's Exhibition "Art Nouveau, 1890–1914"?', *Fashion Theory*, 6/3 (2002)

Thiébaut, Phillipe (ed.), *Art Nouveau Revival: 1900, 1933, 1966, 1974* (Gand: Snoeck/Paris: Musée d'Orsay, 2009)

Thomas, Nicola J., 'Embodying imperial spectacle: Dressing Lady Curzon, Vicereine of India 1899–1905', *Cultural Geographies*, vol. 14/3 (2007)

Tilburg, Patricia, 'Mimi Pinson Goes to War: Taste, Class and Gender in France, 1900–18', *Gender & History*, vol. 23, no. 1 (April 2011)

Troy, Nancy J., *Couture Culture: A Study In Modern Art and Fashion* (Cambridge, Mass./London: MIT Press, 2003)

Ugolini, Laura, *Men and Menswear, Sartorial Consumption in Britain 1880–1939* (Aldershot: Ashgate, 2007)

Verhagen, Marcus, 'The poster in *fin-de-siècle* Paris: "That Mobile and Degenerate Art"' in Charney, Leo and Schwartz, Vanessa R., *Cinema and the Invention of Modern Life* (Berkeley: University of California Press, 1995)

Völker, Angela (with Pichler, Ruperta), *Textiles of the Wiener Werkstätte: 1910–1932* (London: Thames and Hudson, 1994)

Walkley, Christina, *The Way to Wear 'Em: 150 Years of 'Punch' on Fashion* (London: Peter Owen, 1985)

Weimann, Jeanne Madeline, *The Fair Women: The Story of the Woman's Building at the World's Columbian Exposition, Chicago 1893* (Chicago: Academy Chicago, 1981)

Wilcox, Claire and Lister, Jenny (eds), *V&A Gallery of Fashion* (London: V&A, 2013)

Williams, Jean, 'Aquadynamics and the Athletocracy: Jennie Fletcher and the British Women's 4 x 100 metre Freestyle Relay Team at the 1912 Stockholm Olympic Games', *Costume*, vol. 46/2 (June 2012)

Wood, Ghislaine, *Art Nouveau and the Erotic* (London: V&A, 2000)

Wood, Martin A., *Laura Ashley* (London: Frances Lincoln, 2009)

Zapata, Janet, *The Jewelry and Enamels of Louis Comfort Tiffany* (London: Thames and Hudson, 1993)

Primary Sources

'The appanage of the really chic woman, who can wear ankle-bangles incrusted with precious stones', *Illustrated London News*, 25 February 1911, pp.272–3

Austrian Ministry for Public Instruction, *Exhibition of Professional Schools for Arts and Crafts, Universal Exhibition St. Louis 1904* (Vienna: Ministerium für Cultus und Unterricht, 1904)

'British Dress Textiles', *The Times* (London), 27 June 1913, p.21

Commissariat Général du Gouvernement à l'Exposition de Paris de 1900, *Exposition universelle internationale de 1900 à Paris. Section Belge. Catalogue official* (Bruxelles: 1900)

'Contemporary Fashion', *The Times* (London), 22 June 1908, p.6

Cornu, Paul, 'L'Art de la robe', *Art et décoration* (1911)

Les Créateurs de la mode – dessins et documents de Jungbluth, texte de L. Roger-Milès (Paris: Éditions du Figaro/C. Eggiman, 1910)

Desmond, Shaw, 'London Life as seen by Shaw Desmond No.10 – the Picture Palace', *Penny Illustrated Paper* (London), 5 April 1913, p.13

'Earl's Court Exhibition', *The Times* (London), 9 June 1902, p.7

'Exhibition of New Creations for the Autumn Season at Messrs. Woolland Brothers, 95 to 107, Knightsbridge, S.W.', *The Times* (London), 4 October 1909, p.12

'The Franco-British Exhibition', *The Times* (London), 6 June 1908, p.4

'Franco-British Exhibition – Furs and Feathers', *The Times* (London), 22 June 1908, p.16

'French and English Applied Arts', *The Times* (London), 31 October 1908, p.7

Glynn, Prudence, 'Boutiques – or what you will', *The Times*, 23 September 1966, p.15

Grandin, Leon (Mrs), *A Parisienne in Chicago, Impressions of the World's Columbian Exposition* [1893], translated and with an introduction by Mary Beth Raycraft; preface by Arnold Lewis (Urbana, IL: University of Illinois Press, c.2010)

Humphry (Mrs), (of *Truth*) 'The Fashion Exhibits', in Dumas, F.G. (ed.), *The Franco British Exhibition Illustrated Review* (London: Chatto & Windus, 1908)

Loos, Adolf, *Spoken into the Void, Collected Essays 1897–1900* (Cambridge, MA: MIT Press, 1982)

Julius Meier-Graefe, *Die Weltausstellung in Paris 1900* (Leipzig: F. Kruger, 1900)

'Mrs Asquith and French Dresses', *The Times* (London), 15 May 1909, p.13

'Newest "Bakst Minaret"', *Evening Herald* (Klamath Falls, Oregon), 23 February 1914, p.3

'On Parade in Portobello Road: Traders meet boys' demand for military fashion', *The Times* (London), 23 September 1966, p.15

'The Paris Exhibition,' *Morning Post* (London), 3 May 1900, p.5

Poiret, Paul (translated by Stephen Haden Guest), *King of Fashion* [1930] (London: V&A, 2009)

Rau, William H., *Louisiana Purchase Exposition* (Saint Louis, MO: Official Photographic Company of the Louisiana Purchase Exposition, 1904)

'Redfern' (advertisement), *The Times* (London), 6 July 1908, p.12

Shaw, Marian, *World's Fair Notes: A Woman Journalist Views Chicago's 1893 Columbian Exposition* (St Paul, MN: Pogo Press, 1992 [1893])

'Toilettes and Furs in Paris', *The Times* (London), 30 October 1911, p.12

Les Toilettes de la collectivité de la Couture, Exposition universelle internationale de 1900 (Paris: Société de publications d'art, 1900)

Vallance, Aymer, 'British Jewellery and Fans', in Mourey, Gabriel and Vallance, Aymer (eds), *Art Nouveau Jewellery & Fans* [1902] (New York: Dover Publications, 1973)

Wade, Stuart C., *A Week at the Fair: Illustrating Exhibits and Wonders of the World's Columbian Exposition* (Chicago: Rand, McNally & Company, Publishers, 1893)

ACKNOWLEDGEMENTS

—

Many people have helped with the research for this book; I would like to acknowledge particularly Hugh Alexander at The National Archives, Eva White at the Archive of Art and Design and Frances Rankine at the Prints and Drawings Study Room of the V&A for highlighting unpublished documents in their archives. Catherine Polley and the staff of Winchester School of Art Library were extremely helpful with access to secondary literature. I would also like to thank Sue Ralph of Bath Spa University for sharing her research on Margaine-Lacroix. Discussions with Lesley Miller, Edwina Ehrman and Jenny Lister in the Department of Furniture, Textiles and Fashion at the V&A helped to clarify and define the topic of Art Nouveau Fashion. In V&A Publishing, I would like to thank Mark Eastment for his support for this project from an early stage, and Philip Contos for his unfailing patience allied to clear editorial judgement, along with Rachel Malig for her meticulous proofing and Rachel Daley for her picture research. I would also like to thank Jo Banham and the staff at the V&A's Learning department for encouraging me to present my research to live audiences.

At home I have been supported and encouraged by friends and family. This book is dedicated to Rosemary Rose and Rosemary Brook-Hart, who helped me to understand the world of fashion before 1914 – and its relevance today.

PICTURE CREDITS

—

(by plate number)

12	Gift of Miss Eva Drexel Dahlgren, 1976. Photograph by Sheldon Collins © 2014 The Metropolitan Museum of Art/Art Resource/Scala Florence
20	Purchase, Friends of The Costume Institute Gifts, 2005. © 2014 The Metropolitan Museum of Art/Art Resource/Scala, Florence
25	The Jacqueline Loewe Fowler Costume Collection. Gift of Jacqueline Loewe Fowler, 1981. © 2014 The Metropolitan Museum of Art/Art Resource/Scala, Florence
31	© Calouste Gulbenkian Foundation, Lisbon, Photograph by Carlos Azevedo
45	National Archives, Kew
50	House of Worth, London, UK/The Bridgeman Art Library
59	© Ministère de la Culture – Médiathèque du Patrimoine, Dist. RMN-Grand Palais/Atelier de Nadar
61	National Portrait Gallery, London
62	© Chicago History Museum
63	© Chicago History Museum. Photograph by Matthew J. Steffens
64	© Nasjonalmuseet for kunst, arkitektur og design; Stiftelsen Kunstindustrimuseet i Oslo. Teigens Fotoatelier AS
66	National Portrait Gallery, London
68	© L. Degrâces et Ph. Joffre/Galliera/Roger-Viollet
70	Brooklyn Museum Costume Collection at The Metropolitan Museum of Art, Gift of the Brooklyn Museum, 2009. Gift of Mercedes de Acosta, 1954. © 2014 The Metropolitan Museum of Art/Art Resource/Scala, Florence
91	© RMN-Grand Palais (Musée d'Orsay)/Hervé Lewandowski
93	Sakai City Collection
97	National Archives, Kew
105	© Manchester City Galleries. Courtesy of Janet Boston
108	Wien Museum
111, 112	MAK-Austrian Museum of Applied Arts/Contemporary Art. Photo: © MAK
120	Liberty Art Fabrics